# Dwayne's Guitar Lessons Presents:

# Beginner's Guide to Guitar Mode Mastery

By
Guitar Teacher
Dwayne Jenkins

# Introduction

The "Beginner's Guide to Guitar Mode Mastery" is a comprehensive resource designed to elevate your guitar playing through the exploration of modes. Modes are musical scales that form the backbone of countless compositions.

Whether you're just starting or a seasoned player looking to expand your musical vocabulary, mastering the modes can unlock new creative possibilities and deepen your appreciation for the guitar's expressive potential.

While many guitarists are familiar with the basic major and minor scales, modes offer a more nuanced way to understand and use these scales to create harmonious musical landscapes.

Each mode offers a distinct mood and color, from the bright and joyful Ionian mode to the exotic and mysterious Phrygian. By learning how to use modes effectively, you'll be able to convey a wide range of emotions.

This guide is structured to introduce you to each mode, explain its characteristics, and provide practical exercises to help you integrate these concepts into your playing.  As you embark on this journey to mode mastery,

Designed to be accessible and engaging, with clear explanations and exercises tailored for guitarists of all levels. You'll gain insights into the language of music that will enhance your skills.

Whether you're interested in composing original pieces, enhancing your improvisation skills, or simply expanding your musical knowledge, this guide will serve as your roadmap. Allowing you to become a more expressive guitarist.

So grab your guitar and dive into the world of guitar modes. Learn the secrets needed to unlock the mysteries that'll take your guitar playing to the next level.


Sincerely, Dwayne Jenkins

# Table of Contents


Introduction

## Chapter I:  The Ionian Mode  1

Lesson 1:  Introduction to the Ionian Mode  1
Lesson 2:  The Ionian Mode in Different Keys  4
Lesson 3:  Ionian Mode Phrasing  7
Lesson 4:  Chords Within the Ionian Mode  11
Chapter I:  Summary  14

## Chapter II: The Dorian Mode  15

Lesson 5:  Introduction to the Dorian Mode  15
Lesson 6:  Dorian Mode in Different Keys 18
Lesson 7:  Dorian Mode Phrasing  22
Lesson 8:  Chords Within the Dorian Mode  27
Chapter II:  Summary  30

## Chapter III: The Phrygian Mode  31

Lesson 9:  Introduction to the Phrygian Mode  31
Lesson 10:  Phrygian Mode in Different Keys  35
Lesson 11:  Phrygian Mode Phrasing  39
Lesson 12:  Chords Within the Phrygian Mode  43
Chapter III:  Summary  46

## Chapter IV: The Lydian Mode  47

Lesson 13:  Introduction to the Lydian Mode  47
Lesson 14:  Lydian Mode in Different Keys  51
Lesson 15:  Lydian Mode Phrasing  55
Lesson 16:  Chords Within the Lydian Mode  59
Chapter IV:  Summary  62

## Chapter V: The Mixolydian Mode 63

Lesson 17:  Introduction to the Mixolydian Mode 63
Lesson 18:  Mixolydian Mode in Different Keys  67
Lesson 19:  Mixolydian Mode Phrasing  71
Lesson 20:  Chords Within the Mixolydian  75
Chapter V:  Summary  78

**Chapter VI: The Aeolian Mode** 79

Lesson 21:  Introduction to the Aeolian Mode  79
Lesson 22:  Aeolian Mode in Different Keys  83
Lesson 23:  Aeolian Mode Phrasing  86
Lesson 24:  Chords Within the Aeolian  89
Chapter VI:  Summary  92

**Chapter VII: The Locrian Mode** 93

Lesson 25:  Introduction to the Locrian Mode  93
Lesson 26:  Locrian Mode in Different Keys  96
Lesson 27:  Locrian Mode Phrasing  100
Lesson 28:  Chords Within the Locrian  103
Chapter VII:  Summary  106

**Chapter VIII: Additional Concepts  107**

Lesson 29:  Mixing the Modes  107
Lesson 30:  Improvising with the Modes 112
Lesson 31:  Composing with Modes 116
Lesson 32:  Ear Training with the Modes 119
Lesson 33:  Effective Practice Habits  123
Chapter VIII:  Summary  126


Guitar Mode Mastery: Conclusion  127

# Chapter I:  The Ionian Mode

## Lesson 1:  Introduction to the Ionian Mode

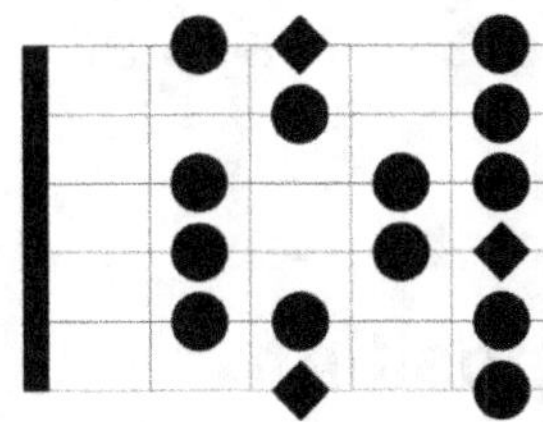

The Ionian mode, also known as the major scale, is one of the most fundamental scales in Western music. It consists of seven notes, serves as the foundation for all other scales, and appears in many musical genres.

The sequence of notes in the Ionian mode follows a specific pattern of whole steps and half steps.  This gives the Ionian mode its distinctive sound and is often associated with a bright, happy tone. A whole step is two frets, and a half step is one.

**Characteristics of the Ionian Sound**

The mode's structure provides a natural sense of balance and completion, making it a popular choice.  The whole step, half step formula for the major scale (Ionian Mode) is:

2

1-W–2–W–3–H–4–W–5–W–6–W–7—H–Octave

If you use this formula, it will give you the notes for any major scale.  This is because they all follow the same scientific formula.  Master the formula, and you'll master the notes to all major scales.

**Building block for music theory and composition.**

- **Structure and Scale Degrees:** The Ionian mode is built on the first degree of the major scale, which consists of seven notes.

Often labeled as degrees **(I, II, III, IV, V, VI, VII)**, with each degree playing a specific role in the scale's harmony.

- **First, Third, and Fifth:** The first, third, and fifth scale degrees are pivotal in establishing the key as major and providing harmonic stability.

The first acts as the home base, while the third determines the major, and the 5th creates tension that resolves back to the first.  This is essential in making major triads.

**A versatile choice for various musical genres.**

With its bright, happy, uplifting sound, the Ionian mode creates a balanced structure that supports smooth, melodic lines and harmonies.  This makes an excellent starting point for mastering and building upon.

Here are a few other things to consider when studying the Ionian mode.

- **The Musical Alphabet:** The twelve notes that are the foundation of all Western music.  A through G sharp.  All scales, chords, and modes will come from these notes.

A–A#--B–C–D–D#--E–F–F#--G–G#

- **Seven Notes From Twelve:** From the twelve notes of the music alphabet, you take seven to make up the major scale or the Ionian mode.  These are the notes that make up the whole-step and half-step formulas.

C–W–D–W–E–H–F–W–G–W–A–W–B–H–Octave

Understanding the Ionian mode's characteristics will help you utilize it effectively in your guitar playing.

4

## Lesson 2:  The Ionian Mode in Different Keys

Transposing the Ionian mode lets you play it in different keys, expanding your knowledge of the fretboard and your versatility as a guitarist. To transpose the Ionian mode, follow these steps:

**Transposing the Ionian Mode**

- **Identify the Key:** Determine the key you wish to transpose the Ionian mode to. For instance, if you're moving from C Ionian to G Ionian, G becomes your new tonic.

This is where knowing your notes along the guitar fretboard comes in handy.

- **Apply the Whole and Half Step Pattern:** Use the whole and half step sequence of the Ionian mode: whole, whole, half, whole, whole, whole, half.

Start with your new tonic and follow this pattern to find the mode's notes in the new key.

- **Practice in Multiple Keys:** Practice the Ionian mode in various keys to enhance your familiarity with the fretboard.

This will improve your ability to play in any musical context, whether accompanying others or improvising.

## Exercises for Mastering Ionian Mode in Different Keys

To become proficient in playing the Ionian mode across different keys, incorporate exercises into your daily practice routine.

- **Key Transposition Exercise:** Choose a starting key and play the Ionian mode. Then, shift to another key and play the mode again.

By doing this, you'll become familiar with the mode.

- **Fretboard Familiarity Drill:** Select a key and play the Ionian mode in different positions along the fretboard. This exercise will deepen your understanding of the neck and improve your ability to navigate between keys.

Continue this process through all 12 keys, focusing on accuracy and fluency.  This will allow you understand the note structure.

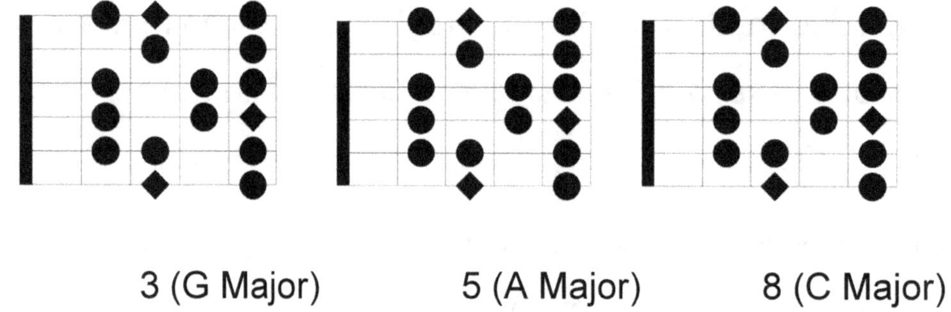

3 (G Major)      5 (A Major)      8 (C Major)

In the examples above, the Ionian mode is played in three keys. G major at the third fret, A major at the 5th fret, and C major at the 8th fret. Note that the pattern remains the same; only the location changes.

This makes it easier to master the notes by seeing them in a pattern. Once that's done, you just need to master where to play it within any key. Say, D major, B major, or F# Major.

By mastering the Ionian mode in different keys, you'll expand your musical repertoire and gain the confidence to perform effectively in any musical setting.

Remember, the Ionian mode sets the tone for all the others, so take time to fully understand it and use it to build a solid foundation.

## Lesson 3:  Ionian Mode Phrasing

Creating effective melodic phrases in the Ionian mode requires an understanding of its bright, harmonious characteristics. Here are some strategies to enhance your melodic phrasing:

### Melodic Phrasing in the Ionian Mode

Once you know the scale pattern well (hopefully by now you do), you can use techniques such as hammer-ons, pull-offs, bends, slides, and vibrato to create phrasing in the mode.

In this first phrasing example, you use pull-offs to achieve a legato feel.  Notice how the phrase repeats itself and ends on the 4th fret with vibrato.  Vibrato is an effective technique for ending a phrase.

A pull-off (if you don't know), is when you pick a note and pull off ot the one behind it.

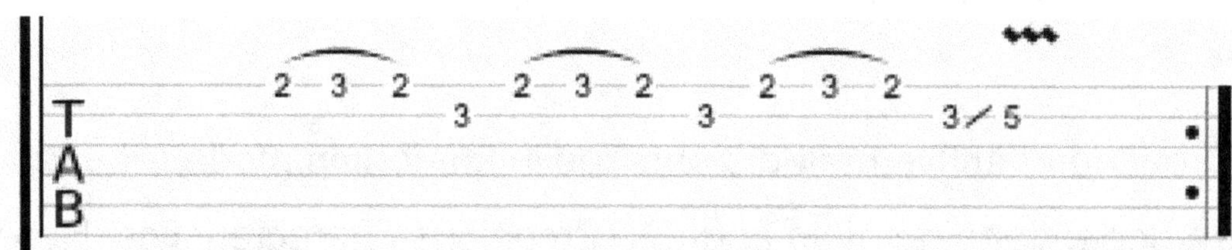

In this second phrasing example, you use a hammer-on, pull-off in a repeated lick three times.  Then slide from the 3 to the 5 and end the phrase with vibrato.

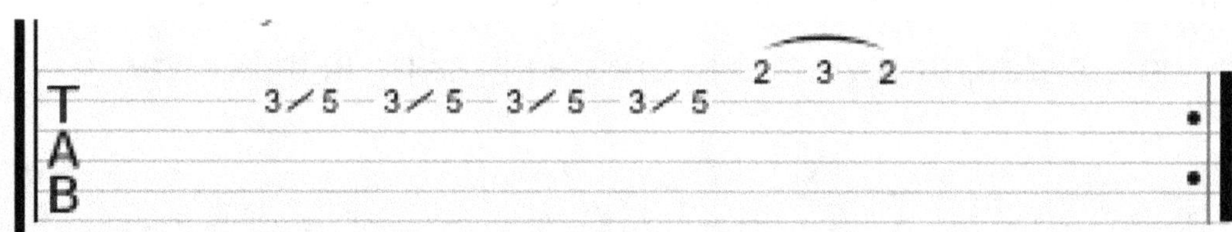

In this third phrasing example, you slide from the 3rd to the 5th repeatedly four times and finish the phrase with a hammer-on pull-off.

When sliding, pick a note and hold it down while sliding to the next note.  Work on sliding both up and down to notes.  This will help you express your notes more effectively and refine this essential technique.

Make sure to do it slowly and for short intervals.  This will get your finger used to the technique.

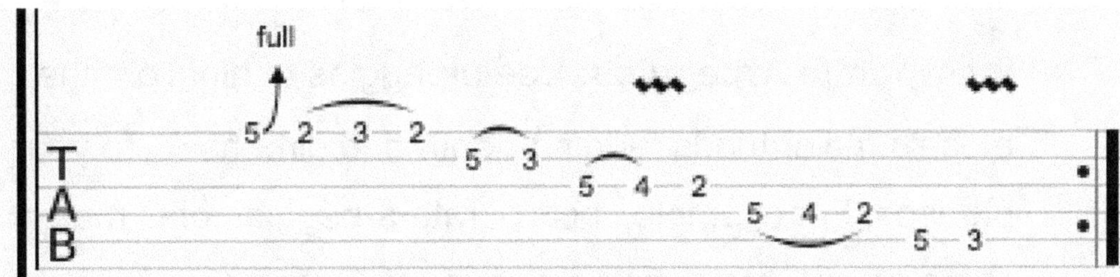


This fourth example of phrasing begins with a string bend.  You pick the string and bend it up.  Then, proceed with hammer-on pull-offs and add vibrato at the 4th fret and 3rd fret.

This will break up the phrase slightly and give it a cadence as you deliver it.

Bending strings is another essential technique in phrasing. String bends can allow you to express a note in many different ways.  I recommend you work on them daily for the best results.

Remember, phrasing is like you talking or singing with your guitar, and the modes and scales that you learn make up the context that you do it in.  Instead of with words, you do it with notes.

The better you are at knowing the pattern of notes and being able to express them with string bends, hammer-ons, slides, pull-offs, vibrato, and so forth, the better you'll be at soloing.

## Additional Ideas For Developing Melodic Phrasing

- **Incorporate Arpeggios:** Use arpeggios to highlight the mode's major triads, adding depth and dimension to your phrases. For example, incorporate arpeggios of C major, G major, or F major when working in C Ionian.

This will help you become more familiar with the mode and the chords it can create.

- **Experiment with Dynamics:** Vary the dynamics within your phrases to add expressiveness. Emphasize certain notes or passages to convey emotions such as joy or triumph.

This is where the techniques discussed earlier come in. Mastering the techniques mentioned earlier, you can express and control the dynamics of the notes.

By mastering these phrasing techniques, you'll be able to create memorable, engaging melodies in the Ionian mode, enriching your musical expression and performance.  Review the ones presented and create your own.

## Lesson 4:  Chords Within the Ionian Mode

In addition to melody, the Ionian mode is a powerful tool for understanding chord construction and harmony. By mastering the chords within the Ionian mode, you can create music that is rich, balanced, and harmonically satisfying.

**Constructing Chords in the Ionian Mode**

The Ionian mode is built on a series of seven notes, each of which can serve as the root of a chord. The chords are constructed by stacking thirds on top of each note, following the interval pattern of the mode. Here's how the chords are constructed in the Ionian mode:

- **I (Tonic) -** Major Chord: The tonic chord is a major chord built on the first scale degree. It establishes the key and provides a sense of home and resolution. For example, in C Ionian, the tonic chord is C major (C-E-G).

These are the 1st, 3rd, and 5th notes of the C major scale.

Key of C Major:  C  D  E  F  G  A  B

- **ii (Supertonic)** - Minor Chord: The supertonic chord is a minor chord built on the second scale degree. It often serves as the dominant's leading chord, preparing for the dominant. In C Ionian, it is D minor (D-F-A).

In the minor scale, the 3rd note is flattened by one fret.  So the F note represents the flat 3rd.

Key of D minor:  D-w-E-h-F-w-G-w-A-h-Bb-w-C-w-Octave.

- **iii (Mediant)** - Minor Chord: The mediant chord is a minor chord built on the third scale degree, lending an emotional and introspective quality. In C Ionian, this is E minor (E-G-B).

Key of E minor:  E-w-F#-h-G-w-A-w-B-h-C-w-D-w-Octave.

- **IV (Subdominant)** - Major Chord: The subdominant chord is a major chord built on the fourth scale degree. It provides movement away from the tonic, often leading to the dominant. In C Ionian, this is F major (F-A-C).

Key of F major:  F-w-G-w-A-h-B flat-w-C-w-D-w-E-h-Octave.

- **V (Dominant)** - Major Chord: The dominant chord is a major chord built on the fifth scale degree and is crucial for creating tension that resolves back to the tonic. It often includes a seventh to increase tension. In C Ionian, this is G major (G-B-D) or G7 (G-B-D-F).

Key of G major:  G-w-A-w-B-h-C-w-D-w-E-w-F#-h-Octave.

- **vi (Submediant)** - Minor Chord: The submediant chord is a minor chord built on the sixth scale degree, frequently used in progressions that evoke emotion. In C Ionian, this is A minor (A-C-E).

Key of A minor:  A-w-B-h-C-w-D-w-E-h-F-w-G-w-Octave.

- **vii (Leading Tone)** - Diminished Chord: The leading tone chord is a diminished chord built on the seventh scale degree. It creates tension and often resolves to the tonic. In C Ionian, this is B diminished (B-D-F).

The diminished will always be made of the 1, 3, and flat 5.

By mastering the major and minor note formulas (and diminished too), you can create music within the Ionian mode that is harmonious and emotional.

14

## Chapter I Summary

<u>First</u>, you are introduced to the Ionian mode.  Also known as the major scale, it is one of the most widely used scales in Western music.  It consists of seven notes and serves as the foundation for all other scales.

<u>Second,</u> you learn about transposition, which moves the mode into different musical keys. This allows you to expand your knowledge of the fretboard and enhance your skills as a guitarist.

<u>Third</u>, you learn about phrasing with the Ionian mode. This is where you bring the scale to life and make it sound like music. This allows you to bring out its bright, harmonious character, enhancing the music you create with it.

<u>Fourth</u>, the Ionian mode is a powerful tool for understanding chord construction and harmony.  By mastering chords within the Ionian mode, you can create music that is rich, balanced, and harmonically satisfying.

<u>Lastly</u>, the Ionian mode is the first of the seven modes and serves as the foundation. It is a major mode, and consists of the w-w-h-w-w-w-h formula.  Master this formula, how to phrase with it, and the chords within it.

# Chapter II: The Dorian Mode

## Lesson 5:  Introduction to the Dorian Modes

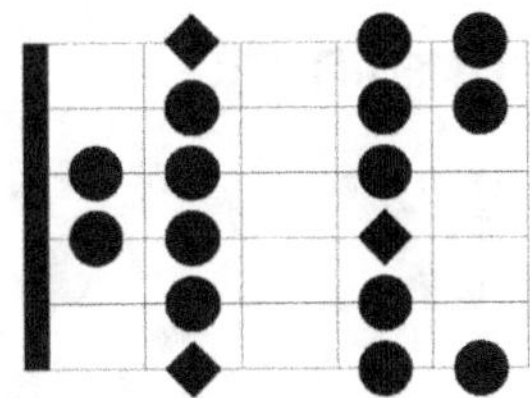

The Dorian mode is the second of the seven musical modes and is often described as a minor scale with a unique twist. It is similar to the natural minor scale but features a raised sixth, which gives it a distinct sound.

## Understanding the Dorian Mode

The Dorian mode is constructed by starting on the second degree of the major scale and follows a pattern of whole and half steps, but it differs from the major scale.  This difference gives the Dorian mode its distinctive minor character, with a major sixth, creating a sound that is both familiar and fresh.

- **Scale Degrees and Structure:** The Dorian mode consists of seven notes, labeled as degrees (I, II, III, IV, V, VI, VII).

Built on the second degree of the major scale, with the major sixth degree being a crucial feature that makes it different.

- **Tonic and Dominant Roles:** The tonic in the Dorian mode serves as the home base, while the dominant creates tension that resolves back to the tonic.

## Characteristics of the Dorian Sound

The Dorian mode's sound is often described as soulful, smooth, and slightly jazzy. Its unique interval structure allows it to convey a wide range of emotions, from introspection to optimism.

- **Emotional Qualities:** The Dorian mode is known for its balance of minor tonality with a touch of brightness, thanks to the major sixth.

This combination makes it ideal for genres like jazz, blues, and folk, where a nuanced emotional palette is desired.

- **Common Usage:** The Dorian mode is frequently used in jazz improvisation, modal jazz compositions, blues, and in rock and folk music.

- **Melodic and Harmonic Flexibility:** The Dorian mode's structure allows for fluid melodic lines and rich harmonic textures.

Its characteristic intervals provide a flexible foundation for crafting expressive melodies and complex chord progressions.

Ionian Mode:  1  2  3  4  5  6  7

Dorian Mode:  1  2  b3  4  5  6  b7

Notice the difference between the two modes; it is this difference that gives them their individual character.  It is this character that you want to explore and exploit.

- **Understanding the structure:** The characteristics of the Dorian mode provide valuable insights into its expressive potential and versatility.

This foundational knowledge will enhance your ability to create and perform music that resonates with depth and emotional richness.  Making you a much better guitarist and composer.

## Lesson 6:  The Dorian Mode in Different Keys

Transposing the Dorian mode to different keys is a valuable skill that enhances your guitar versatility. Understanding this allows you to play the Dorian mode in any musical context, expanding your improvisational and compositional abilities.

**Transposing the Dorian Mode**

- **Identify the Key:** Determine the tonic (root note) of the key to which you want to transpose the Dorian mode. For example, if you are moving from D Dorian to A Dorian, A becomes your new tonic.

Key of A Dorian:  A-w-B-h-C-w-D-w-E-w-F#-h-G-w-Octave

- **Apply the Whole and Half Step Pattern:** Follow the Dorian mode's specific pattern: whole, half, whole, whole, whole, half, whole.

Start from your new tonic and apply this sequence to find the notes of the Dorian mode in the new key.

Key of D Dorian:  D-w-E-h-F-w-G-w-A-w-B-h-C-w-Octave.

Key of G Dorian:  G-w-A-h-Bb-w-C-w-D-w-E-h-F-w-Octave.

**Exercises for Mastering Dorian Mode in Different Keys**

To become proficient in playing the Dorian mode across different keys, work daily at incorporating the following exercises into your practice routine:

- **Key Transposition Challenge:** Select a starting key and play the Dorian mode. Shift to another key and play the mode again.

Continue this process across all 12 keys, following the examples presented, with a focus on accuracy and smooth transitions.

- **Fretboard Navigation Drill:** Choose a key and play the Dorian mode in different positions along the fretboard.

This exercise will deepen your understanding of the neck and enhance your ability to move between keys effortlessly.

Key of F Dorian:  F-w-G-h-Ab-w-Bb-w-C-w-D-h-Eb-w-Octave.

Key of C Dorian:  C-w-D-h-Eb-w-F-w-G-w-A-h-Bb-w-Octave.

- **Harmonization Practice:** In your selected key, harmonize the Dorian mode by playing chords built on each scale degree.

This will improve your understanding of how the notes relate harmonically within the mode.

1. **Work with Backing Tracks:** use tracks in various keys and explore the Dorian mode. This exercise will develop your ear and visualization skills, making you a more flexible and creative guitarist.

Remember, you want to be able to see the notes of the mode as they lie along the fretboard.  This is why you learn them in patterns.  If you can visualize and think in patterns, you will excel in your learning.

All scales on the fretboard (modes included) can be broken down into patterns.  Master the pattern and its location in specific keys, and you will unlock the mysteries of the fretboard.

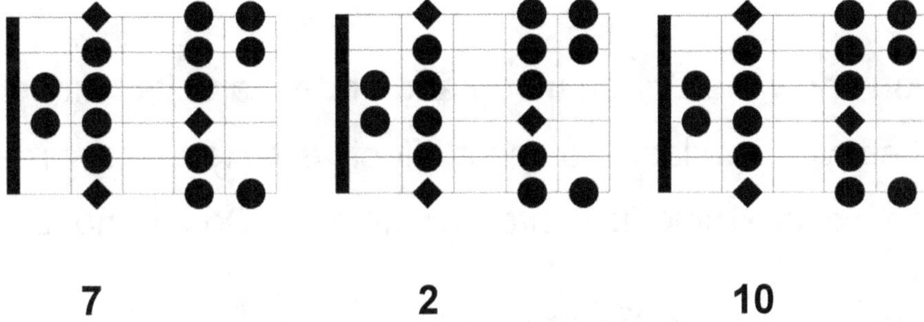



What keys are these in?  This is what you want to master. Seeing the mode in the box pattern, and knowing where it is along the fretboard in any key.

D Dorian is in what major key?

F# Dorian is in what major key?

C Dorian is in what major Key?

The more you look at the box pattern and go through it in different keys along the fretboard, the more you will be able to answer these questions quickly.

By mastering the Dorian mode in different keys, you'll expand your musical repertoire and gain confidence in performing across diverse musical settings.

22

## Lesson 7:  Dorian Mode Phrasing

Now that you know the Dorian mode and understand its unique tonal qualities, you can learn to use it effectively. Here are some strategies to explore melodic contours within the Dorian mode:

**Dorian Mode Phrasing Examples**

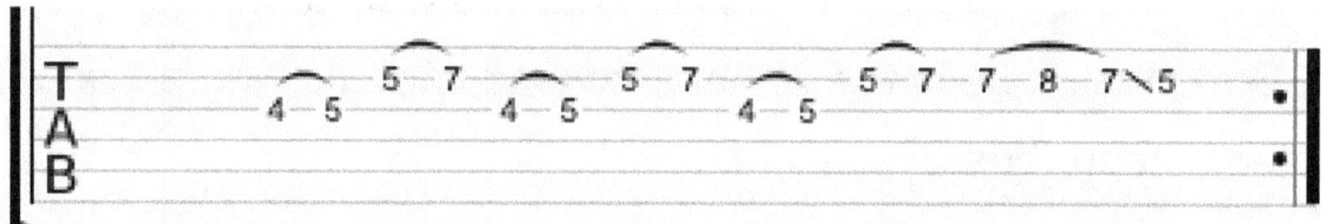

In this first phrasing example, hammer-ons are utilized with a slide at the end.

In this second example, double pull-offs are used in a legato fashion with a pull-off into a slide, and vibrato at the end.

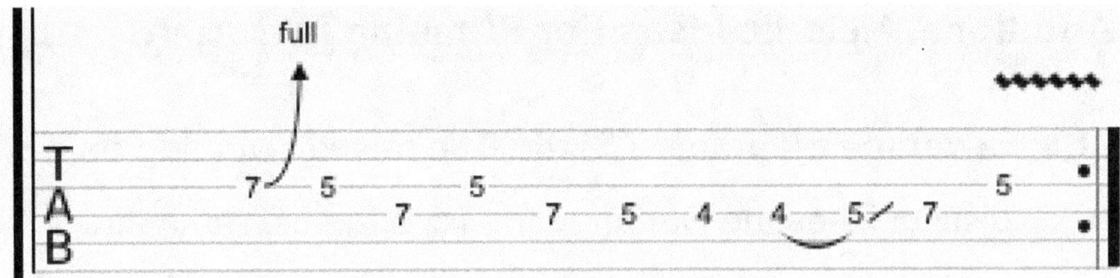

In this third example, you start with a bend, move through the mode, perform a smooth hammer-on, slide, and end with a vibrato.

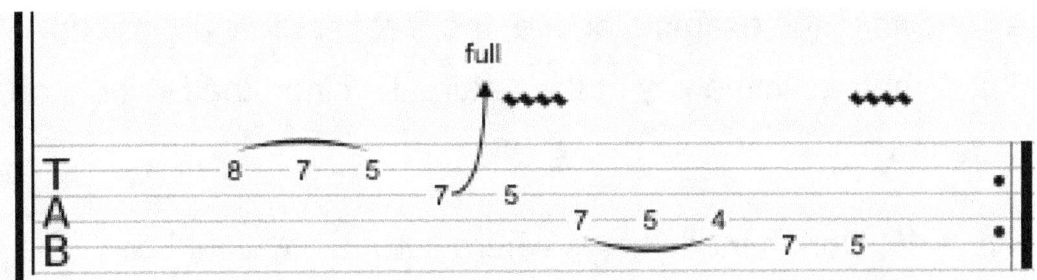

In this fourth example, you start with a double pull-off and do a string bend with vibrato.  Then a similar lick without a bend, ending with a vibrato.

Remember, hammer-ons, pull-offs, bends, slides, vibrato, and so forth are what are used to create phrasing.  Learn the techniques individually, then put them together to craft memorable musical landscapes.

## Additional Melodic Ideas For Phrasing in Dorian

- **Leverage the Raised Sixth:** The raised sixth degree distinguishes the Dorian mode from the natural minor scale, giving it a brighter, more hopeful sound. Emphasize this interval to highlight the mode's distinct character in your melodies.

D Dorian:  D-w-E-h-F-w-G-w-A-w-B-h-C-w-Octave.

As shown in the example above, the B represents the raised 6th.  Whereas in the key of the natural D minor, the B would be flattened.

Since the Dorian mode stays where it normally would be in the key of D major, it is a bit of both major and minor.  Providing a major sixth interval from the root.

- **Incorporate Arpeggiated Patterns:** Arpeggiating chords within the Dorian mode, such as minor triads and seventh chords, adds depth and interest to your melodic phrases.

A Dorian:  A-w-B-h-C-w-D-w-E-w-F#-h-G-w-Octave.

A minor:  A-C-E.  A minor 7th: A-C-E-G.  See how this works?

- **Create Tension and Resolution:** Build tension by ascending to the seventh degree and resolving to the tonic or fifth degree, creating a satisfying closure typical of the Dorian mode.

D Dorian:  D-w-E-h-F-w-G-w-A-w-B-h-C-w-Octave.

An example of tension in the D Dorian is the movement between Dm7 and G7, with G7 providing a brighter quality that stands out compared to Dm7.

## Practicing with the Dorian mode

Practicing in the Dorian mode allows you to explore its soulful, slightly jazzy character. Here are some additional tips to enhance your guitar skills using the Dorian mode:

- **Modal Jam Sessions:** Play along with backing tracks in various keys, focusing on the Dorian mode.

Experiment with different phrasing techniques and melodic ideas to develop your unique musical voice.  Like the phrasing examples presented earlier.

- **Call-and-Response Exercises:** Practice the art of call-and-response with a partner or recording by playing a phrase and responding with a complementary phrase in the Dorian mode.

This exercise helps develop your listening skills and melodic creativity.  Allowing you to prepare to play with others who may take the role of call-and-response.

- **Phrase Development:** Start with a simple melodic idea and gradually develop it by varying the rhythm, dynamics, and note choices.

This approach will help you build engaging and cohesive solos that showcase the Dorian mode's characteristics.

- **Emphasize Harmonic Context:** Pay attention to the underlying chord progression and use the Dorian scale to create melodic lines that complement and enhance the harmony.

By mastering these phrasing techniques, you'll be able to create compelling and expressive music in the Dorian mode, enriching your overall guitar playing and musical expression.

## Lesson 8:  Chords Within the Dorian Mode

The Dorian mode, characterized by its unique blend of minor and major tonalities, offers a rich palette for chord construction. Understanding the chords in the Dorian mode will enhance your ability to create harmonically interesting, soulful music.

### Constructing Chords in the Dorian Mode

The Dorian mode is built on the second degree of the major scale and follows a distinct pattern of whole and half steps: whole, half, whole, whole, whole, half, whole.

Each note in the Dorian scale can serve as the root of a chord, with chords built by stacking thirds on each note. Here's how the chords are constructed in the Dorian mode:

- **I (Tonic)** - Minor Chord: The tonic chord is a minor chord built on the first scale degree. It establishes the key and provides a sense of home. For example, in D Dorian, the tonic chord is D minor (D-F-A).

Key of D minor:  D-w-E-h-F-w-G-w-A-h-Bb-w-C-w-Octave.

- **ii (Supertonic)** - Minor Chord: The supertonic chord is a minor chord built on the second scale degree. It often serves as a transition chord. In D Dorian, it is E minor (E-G-B).

Key of E minor:  E-w-F#-h-G-w-A-w-B-h-C-w-Octave.

- **III (Mediant)** - Major Chord: The mediant chord is a major chord built on the third scale degree, lending brightness and contrast. In D Dorian, this is F major (F-A-C).

Key of F major:  F-w-G-w-A-h-Bb-w-C-w-D-w-E-h-Octave.

- **IV (Subdominant)** - Major Chord: The subdominant chord is a major chord built on the fourth scale degree and adds movement away from the tonic. In D Dorian, this is G major (G-B-D).

Key of G major:  G-w-A-w-B-h-C-w-D-w-E-w-F#-h-Octave.

- **V (Dominant)** - Minor Chord: The dominant chord is a minor chord built on the fifth scale degree, adding tension that resolves back to the tonic. In D Dorian, this is A minor (A-C-E).

Key of A minor:  A-w-B-h-C-w-D-w-E-h-F-w-G-w-Octave.

- **VI (Submediant) -** Diminished Chord: The submediant chord is a diminished chord built on the sixth scale degree, often used to add tension. In D Dorian, this is B diminished (B-D-F).

Remember, the diminished triad includes the flat 5th.

- **VII (Subtonic) -** Major Chord: The subtonic chord is a major chord built on the seventh scale degree, offering a strong resolution to the tonic. In D Dorian, this is C major (C-E-G).

Key of C major:  C-w-D-w-E-h-F-w-G-w-A-w-B-h-Octave.

By mastering these chords and their functions, you can create harmonically rich and expressive music within the Dorian mode. Experiment with different progressions to discover how these chords interact and enhance your compositions.

## Chapter II Summary

<u>First</u>, you are introduced to the Dorian mode.  It is the second mode, and is often described as a minor scale with a unique twist.  It is similar to the natural minor scale but features a raised sixth, giving it a distinct sound.

<u>Second</u>, as with the Ionian, you learn how to transpose it.  Like the Ionian mode, this allows you to enhance your knowledge of the fretboard, as well as increase your musicianship.  The idea here is to play it in multiple musical keys.

<u>Third</u>, you learn about phrasing with the Dorian mode.  Just like with the Ionian mode, this allows you to bring out the character of the mode.  This is done with hammer-ons, pull-offs, slides, bends, and vibrato.

<u>Fourth</u>, you learn about chords that exist within the Dorian mode.  Just like the Ionian, this helps with chord construction and enhances your ability to craft harmonically, soulful music.

<u>Lastly</u>, the Dorian mode is the second of the seven modes and is minor because its lowered third and major sixth.  The note interval formula for the Dorian is w-h-w-w-w-h-w, and should be committed to memory for best results.

# Chapter III: The Phrygian Mode

## Lesson 9:  Introduction to the Phrygian Mode

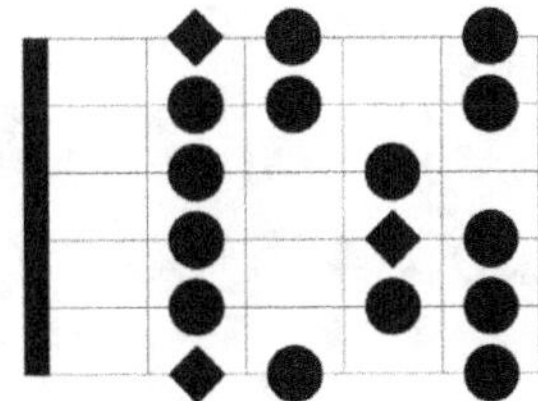

The Phrygian mode is the third of the seven musical modes and is known for its exotic and somewhat mysterious sound. It is similar to the natural minor scale but features a lowered second degree, which gives it a moody character.

### Understanding the Phrygian Mode

Formed by starting on the third degree of the major scale and following a specific interval pattern, this sequence gives the Phrygian mode its distinctive minor quality, with a lowered second degree that sets it apart from the natural minor scale.

G major scale:  G  A  B  C  D  E  F#  Octave

- Scale Degrees and Structure: The Phrygian mode consists of seven notes, labeled as degrees built on the third degree of the major scale; its lowered second degree is a defining feature.

B Phrygian:  B  C  D  E  F  G  A  Octave = 1  b2  b3  4  5  b6  b7

**Characteristics of the Phrygian Sound**

The Phrygian mode is often described as dark, mysterious, and exotic. Its unique interval structure allows it to convey a wide range of emotions, from tension and unease to passion and intensity.

- **Emotional Qualities:** The Phrygian mode's lowered second degree lends it a haunting, somewhat eerie quality that can evoke feelings of tension and mystery.

This makes it ideal for genres such as flamenco, metal, and certain types of jazz.

- **Common Usage:** The Phrygian mode is frequently used in Spanish and Middle Eastern music, as well as in metal and progressive rock.

Its distinctive sound offers a rich palette for musicians looking to explore unconventional tonal landscapes.

- **Melodic and Harmonic Flexibility:** This structure of the Phrygian mode allows for fluid melodic lines and rich harmonic textures.

Its characteristic intervals provide a flexible foundation for crafting expressive melodies and complex chord progressions.

- **Spanish Influence:** The Phrygian mode is deeply associated with Flamenco music and Spanish guitar.

Its distinct intervals, especially the lowered second, contribute to its evocative, passionate sound, reminiscent of traditional Spanish melodies and rhythms.

- **Eastern Flavor:** The Phrygian mode's tonal qualities often evoke a sense of Middle Eastern music.

Its exotic sound palette can transport listeners to distant lands, making it a popular choice for compositions aiming to create an atmosphere of intrigue and adventure.

Harness the Phrygian mode's unique qualities to enrich your compositions and performances with its distinctive sound.

By understanding the structure and characteristics of the Phrygian mode, you'll gain valuable insights into its expressive potential and versatility.

This foundational knowledge will enhance your ability to create and perform music that resonates with depth and emotional richness.

Ionian Mode:  1 2 3 4 5 6 7: (w w h w w w h)

Dorian Mode:  1 2 b3 4 5 6 b7: (w h w w w h w)

Phrygian Mode: 1 b2 b3 4 5 b6 b7:  (h w w w h w w)

*Notice the difference between the three modes.

## Lesson 10:  Phrygian Mode in Different Keys

Exploring the Phrygian mode across various keys expands your musical repertoire and enhances your versatility as a guitarist. Understanding how to transpose this mode allows you to incorporate its exotic sound into your playing, no matter the key.

**Transposing the Phrygian Mode**

Transposing the Phrygian mode requires a grasp of its unique interval structure and how it interacts with different key signatures. Here are the steps to effectively transpose the Phrygian mode:

- **Identify the Root:** Determine the root note of the key in which you wish to play the Phrygian mode. For example, if you're transitioning from E Phrygian to B Phrygian, B becomes your new root.

E Phrygian:  E  F  G  A  B  C  D  Octave

B Phrygian:  B  C  D  E  F sharp  G  A  Octave

- **Apply the Interval Pattern:** Use the Phrygian mode's sequence of whole and half steps: half, whole, whole, whole, half, whole, whole.

Starting from your new tonic, follow this pattern to determine the notes of the mode in the new key.  Remember, the sequence will always be the same; it's just the notes that will change.

- **Practice Across Keys:** Regularly practice the Phrygian mode in different keys to improve your familiarity with the fretboard and your adaptability.

This will enable you to integrate this mode into various musical contexts seamlessly.

A Phrygian Mode:  A-h-Bb-w-C-w-D-w-E-h-F-w-G-w-Octave.

C Phrygian Mode: C-h-Db-w-Eb-w-F-w-G-h-Ab-w-Bn-w-Octave.

D Phrygian Mode:  D-h-Eb-w-F-w-G-w-A-h-Bb-w-C-w-Octave.

G Phrygian Mode:  G-h-Ab-w-Bb-w-C-w-D-h-Eb-w-F-w-Octave.

**Mastering Phrygian Mode in Different Keys**

To gain proficiency in playing the Phrygian mode across multiple keys, incorporate the following exercises into your practice routine:

- **Key Transposition Exercise:** Select a starting key and play the Phrygian mode. Shift to a different key and play the mode again.

Continue this process through all 12 keys, focusing on accuracy and fluency.  This will help you to not only master the mode, but also the fretboard.

- **Fretboard Navigation Drill:** Choose a key and play the Phrygian mode in different positions along the fretboard.

This exercise will deepen your understanding of the neck and improve your ability to move between keys effortlessly.

- **Harmonization Practice:** In your selected key, harmonize the Phrygian mode by playing chords built on each scale degree. This practice enhances your understanding of how the mode's notes relate harmonically.

E Phrygian:  E-h-F-w-G-w-A-w-B-h-C-w-D-w-Octave

E minor:  E  G  B = 1  b3  5

F major:  F  A  C = 1  3  5

These are just a few examples that come out of the E Phrygian. Work with this concept in other keys, and you'll be able to enhance your chord vocabulary and unlock the mysteries of the mode.

- **Work with Backing Tracks:** Use backing tracks in various keys and improvise using the Phrygian mode.

By mastering the Phrygian mode in different keys, you'll expand your musical repertoire, gain confidence in performing across diverse settings, and enhance your overall guitar playing and musical expression.

## Lesson 11:  Phrygian Mode Phrasing

Crafting melodies in the Phrygian mode involves tapping into its exotic and mysterious sound. Here are some strategies to enhance your melodic phrasing within this mode:

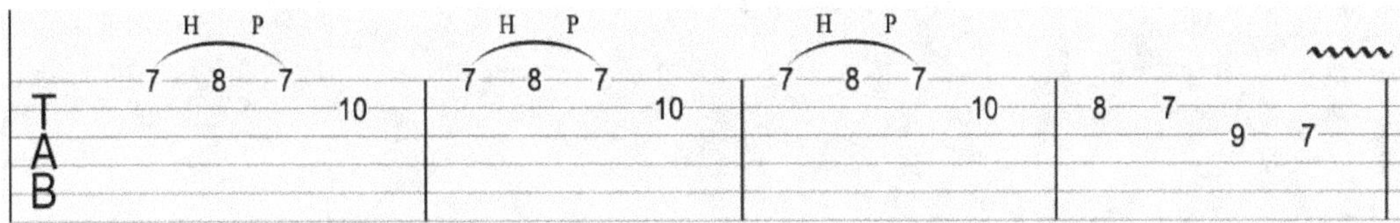

In this first phrasing example, you use hammer-ons and pull-offs, and end the phrase with vibrato.

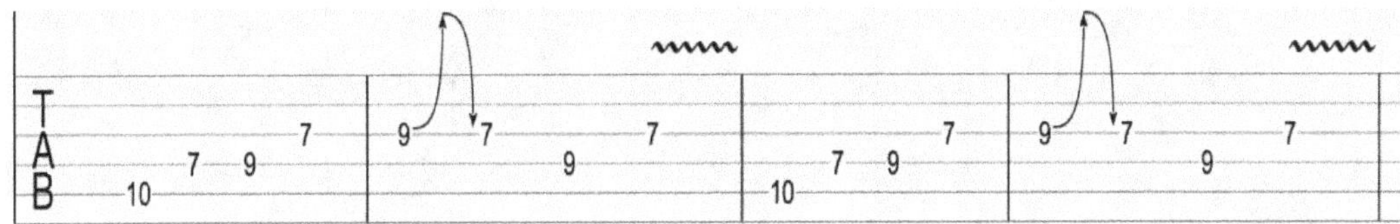

In this example, you go through the mode with a repeated lick using a bend release and vibrato.

Remember, mastering techniques like hammer-ons, pull-offs, bends, and so forth is what will bring the modes to life.  Allow you to bring out each one's character.

In this third example, you repeat a lick for three measures, then change it in the fourth measure, ending with vibrato.

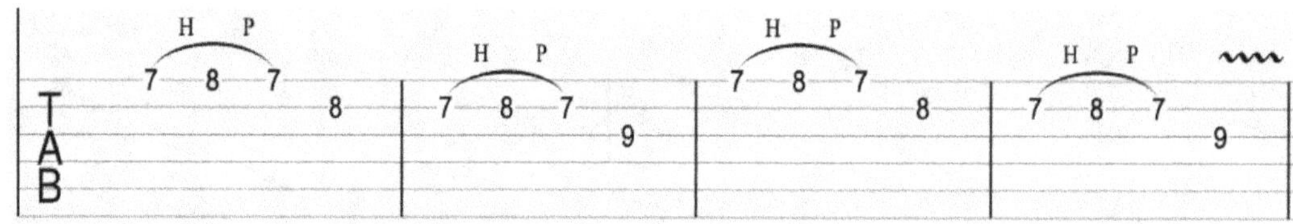

In this fourth example, you utilize the hammer-on pull-off in a repeated lick and end with vibrato.

In this last example, you utilize slides as you go through the mode and end the phrase with vibrato.

Remember, vibrato is a great way to add expression to a note, and it works well at the end of a phrase.

Like the modes before it, work on these phrases, get familiar with the mode, and learn how to get it to sound like music.

## Additional Melodic Phrasing Ideas in Phrygian

- **Emphasize the Lowered Second:** The lowered second degree is the hallmark of the Phrygian mode, imbuing it with a distinct exotic quality.

Highlight this interval in your melodies to capture the mode's unique character.

- **Use Flowing Movement:** The Phrygian mode's interval sequence lends itself well to smooth, flowing melodic lines.

Incorporate stepwise motion to create seamless, captivating phrases that maintain listener interest.

- **Incorporate Rhythmic Variety:** Experiment with diverse rhythmic patterns to add dynamic interest to your melodies.

Syncopation or irregular rhythms can enhance the tension and intrigue typical of Phrygian melodies.

- **Explore Arpeggios:** Use arpeggios to emphasize the mode's minor triads and create depth in your melodic lines.

Arpeggiating chords like E minor or F major in E Phrygian can add texture and complexity.

- **Thumb Independence**: Focus on developing thumb independence so it can maintain a steady bass rhythm while your other fingers play melody or harmony. Practice exercises that isolate thumb movement to strengthen this skill.

## Integrating Phrygian Phrasing Techniques

- **Phrase Variation Exercise:** Take a simple melodic phrase and vary it by altering its rhythm, dynamics, or note choice.

This practice will enhance your ability to create diverse and engaging phrases within the Phrygian mode. By mastering these techniques, you'll be able craft compelling music.

## Lesson 12:  Chords Within the Phrygian Mode

The Phrygian mode, known for its exotic and somewhat mysterious sound, offers a distinctive set of chords that can add depth and intrigue to your music. Enhancing your ability to create harmonically rich compositions.

### Constructing Chords in the Phrygian Mode

The Phrygian mode is built on the third degree of the major scale and is identified by a lowered second degree, which gives it its unique tonal quality.

Each note in the Phrygian scale can serve as the root of a chord, constructed by stacking thirds on top of each note. Here's how the chords are constructed in the Phrygian mode:

- **I (Tonic) -** Minor Chord: The tonic chord is a minor chord built on the first scale degree. It establishes the key and sets the exotic tone of the mode. For example, in E Phrygian, the tonic chord is E minor (E-G-B).

E minor:  E-w-F#-h-G-w-A-w-B-h-C-w-D-w-Octave.

- **bII (Supertonic) -** Major Chord: The supertonic chord is a major chord built on the lowered second scale degree. This chord adds tension and intrigue, contributing to the mode's unique sound. In E Phrygian, this is F major (F-A-C).

F Major:  F-w-G-w-A-h-Bb-w-C-w-D-w-E-h-Octave.

- **bIII (Mediant) -** Major Chord: The mediant chord is a major chord built on the third scale degree, providing a sense of brightness. In E Phrygian, this is G major (G-B-D).

G major:  G-w-A-w-B-h-C-w-D-w-E-w-F#-h-Octave.

- **iv (Subdominant) -** Minor Chord: The subdominant chord is a minor chord built on the fourth scale degree, offering a sense of movement. In E Phrygian, this is A minor (A-C-E).

A minor:  A-w-B-h-C-w-D-w-E-h-F-w-G-w-Octave.

- **v (Dominant) -** Minor Chord: The dominant chord is a minor chord built on the fifth scale degree, adding tension that resolves back to the tonic. In E Phrygian, this is B minor (B-D-F#).

B minor:  B-w-C#-h-D-w-E-w-F#-h-G-w-A-w-Octave.

- **bVI (Submediant) -** Major Chord: The submediant chord is a major chord built on the sixth scale degree, contributing to the mode's rich harmonic palette. In E Phrygian, this is C major (C-E-G).

C major:  C-w-D-w-E-h-F-w-G-w-A-w-B-h-Octave.

- **bVII (Subtonic) -** Major Chord: The subtonic chord is a major chord built on the seventh scale degree, offering a strong resolution to the tonic. In E Phrygian, this is D major (D-Fsharp-A).

D major:  D-w-E-w-F#-h-G-w-A-w-B-w-C#-h-Octave.

By mastering these chords and their functions within the Phrygian mode, you can create music that is harmonically interesting and emotionally resonant.

## Chapter III Summary

First, you are introduced to the Phrygian mode.  The third of the seven modes.  Also, a minor mode.  Known for its exotic and somewhat mysterious sound.  It is similar to the natural minor scale, but features a lowered second.

Second, you focus on transposing the Phrygian mode.  Playing it in different keys allows you to gain fretboard knowledge and enhance your musicianship.  Play it in one key, and be able to move to any other one you wish.

Third, you learn about phrasing with the Phrygian mode.  Just as with the Ionian and Dorian, this allows you to discover and bring out the musical landscape, adding diversity to your compositions.

Fourth, you learn about chords that reside within the mode. This allows you to add depth and intrigue to your music.  The reason for this is that each tone degree within the mode can be used as the root of a chord.

Lastly, the Phrygian mode is the third of the seven and has a unique tone quality due to its lowered second degree added to the natural minor scale.  Its formula is, h-w-w-w-h-w-w.  Like the other modes, this is what you want to master.

# Chapter IV:  The Lydian Mode

## Lesson 13:  Introduction to the Lydian Mode

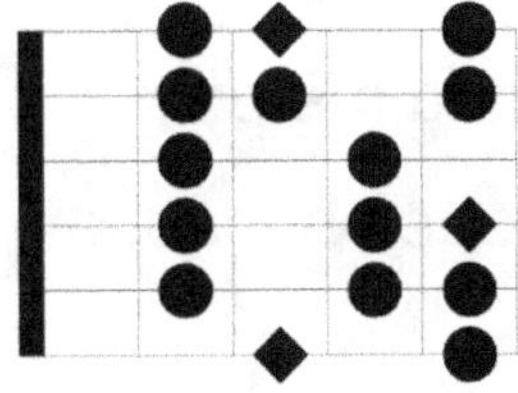

The Lydian mode is the fourth of the seven musical modes and is characterized by its bright, ethereal sound. It is similar to the major scale but features a raised fourth degree, which gives it a distinctive, almost dreamy quality.

### Understanding the Lydian Mode

- **Scale Degrees and Structure:** The Lydian mode consists of seven notes, labeled as degrees (I, II, III, #IV, V, VI, VII).

The raised fourth degree is the defining feature that sets the Lydian mode apart from the Ionian, contributing to its airy, open sound.

- **Root and Dominant Roles:** In the Lydian mode, the root serves as the home base, while the raised fourth degree creates a tension that resolves to the root or other scale degrees.

This relationship is key to the mode's harmonic and melodic movement, making it unique among the other modes because of the raised fourth it shares with no other mode.

## Characteristics of the Lydian Sound

The Lydian mode is often described as bright, ethereal, and otherworldly. Its unique interval structure conveys a sense of wonder and exploration, making it ideal for compositions that seek to inspire and uplift.

- **Emotional Qualities:** The Lydian mode's raised fourth degree imparts an unexpected, magical quality that can evoke feelings of joy, curiosity, and inspiration.

This makes it a preferred choice for genres such as film scores, progressive rock, and jazz fusion.

- **Common Usage:** The Lydian mode is often used in compositions seeking to evoke expansiveness or mysticism.

Its bright, open sound is well-suited for melodies and harmonies that explore new musical landscapes.

- **Melodic and Harmonic Flexibility:** The structure of the Lydian mode allows for fluid melodic lines and rich harmonic textures.

Its characteristic intervals provide a flexible foundation for crafting engaging and innovative compositions.

- **Evoking Wonder:** The Lydian mode is particularly effective at conveying a sense of wonder and possibility.

Its bright intervals and distinctive raised fourth can transport listeners to new and imaginative worlds, making it a powerful tool for musical storytelling.

## Practical Applications of the Lydian Mode

Exploring the practical applications of the Lydian mode can help you incorporate its unique sound into your compositions and performances.

- **Creating Dreamy Soundscapes:** The open, airy sound of the Lydian mode is ideal for crafting atmospheric music.

Layering instruments in the Lydian mode can create lush, ambient soundscapes that transport listeners to otherworldly realms. Experiment with different timbres and textures.

- **Enhancing Rock and Pop Songs:** The Lydian mode's distinctive sound can add a touch of magic to these compositions.

Use it to create memorable hooks or bridge sections that stand out, providing a refreshing contrast to more traditional chord progressions.

By understanding these applications, you'll be equipped to harness their unique qualities in your musical endeavors.

## Lesson 14: Lydian Mode in Different Keys

Transposing the Lydian mode to different keys is a crucial skill for any guitarist looking to explore its bright and ethereal sound across diverse musical contexts.

**Transposing the Lydian Mode**

- **Identify the Tonic:** Determine the root note of the key you want to transpose to.

For example, if you're shifting from C Lydian to G Lydian, G becomes your new tonic.

C Lydian:  C  D  E  F#  G  A  B = 1  2  3  #4  5  6  7

G Lydian:  G  A  B  C#  D  E  F# = 1  2  3  #4  5  6  7

- **Apply the Whole and Half Step Pattern:** The Lydian mode follows this sequence: whole, whole, whole, half, whole, whole, half.

Start from your new tonic and apply this pattern to identify the scale notes in the new key.

- **Practice in Multiple Keys:** Regularly practice the Lydian mode in various keys to develop a deeper understanding of the fretboard.

This skill will enhance your ability to incorporate the Lydian sound into your improvisation and composition across different musical settings.

## Lydian Mode Exercises in Different Keys

To gain proficiency in playing the Lydian mode across multiple keys, include the following exercises in your practice routine:

- **Key Transposition Exercise:** Choose a starting key and play the Lydian mode. Shift to another key and play the mode again.

By continuing this process throughout the fretboard, you not only get to know the mode intimately.

- **Fretboard Navigation Drill:** Select a key and play the Lydian mode in different positions along the fretboard.

This exercise will deepen your understanding of the neck and improve your ability to move between keys effortlessly.

- **Harmonization Practice:** In your chosen key, harmonize the Lydian mode by playing chords built on each scale degree.

This will help you understand the chords within the mode and how the mode's notes relate harmonically.

- **Work with Backing Tracks:** Use backing tracks in various keys and improvise using the Lydian mode.

This exercise will develop your ear and timing skills, making you a more flexible and creative guitarist.

## Techniques for Modal Interchange

- **Identify Parallel Modes:** Begin by identifying parallel modes that share the same tonic note but differ in their scale degrees.

For example, C Ionian (major) and C Lydian share the same tonic but differ in their raised fourth degree.

C Ionian: C D E F G A B = 1 2 3 4 5 6 7

C Lydian: C D E F# G A B = 1 2 3 #4 5 6 7

- **Borrowing Chords:** Experiment with incorporating chords from these parallel modes into your compositions.

For instance, in a C major progression, try using an Fsharp diminished chord from C Lydian to introduce a new color and tension.

C Lydian:  C  D  E  F#  G  A  B = 1  2  3  #4  5  6  7

F sharp diminished chord:  F#  A  C =  1  b3  b5

*Notice how this chord resides within the Lydian mode.

- **Create Contrast:** Utilize modal interchange to create contrast within your compositions.

For example, a shift from a bright, stable Ionian section to a more mysterious, unresolved Phrygian section can evoke different emotional responses.

By mastering the Lydian mode across different keys, you'll expand your musical repertoire and gain confidence performing in diverse settings, enriching your overall guitar playing and musical expression.

## Lesson 15:  Lydian Mode Phrasing

The Lydian mode, with its distinctive raised fourth, offers a
bright and expansive palette for creating captivating melodies.
To harness the ethereal quality of the Lydian mode, utilize the
same techniques as you did in the previous modes.

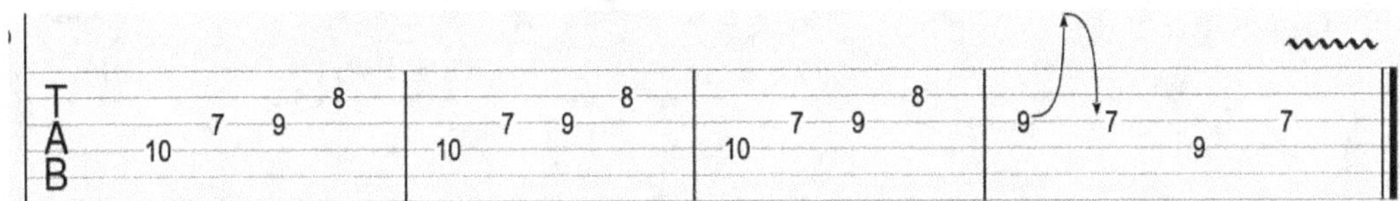

In this first phrasing example, you do a simple four-note
repeated lick for three measures, add a bend release, and finish
with a vibrato.

In this second example, you utilize the bend release again with
vibrato, pull-off hammer-on, and a repeated lick.

Remember, these are the types of techniques that express the
character within the modes.

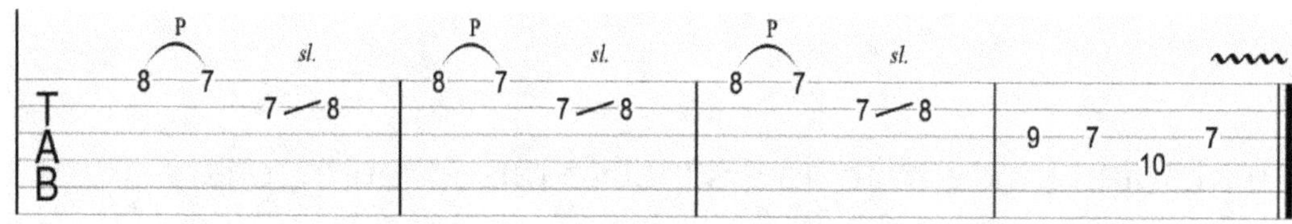

In this third example, you play repeated licks using pull-offs, slides, and vibrato.

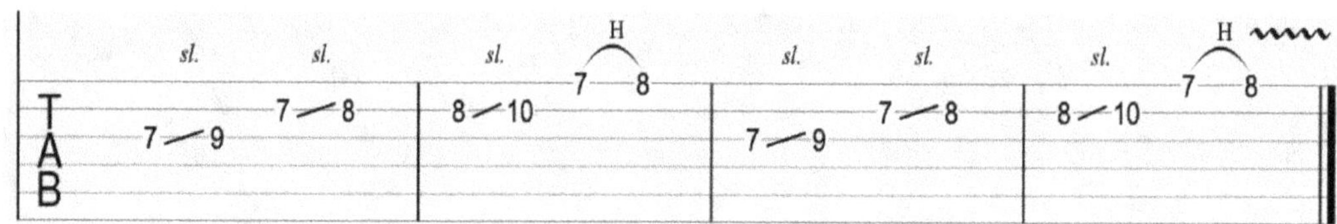

In this fourth example, you use another repeated lick with sides, hammer-ons, and vibrato.

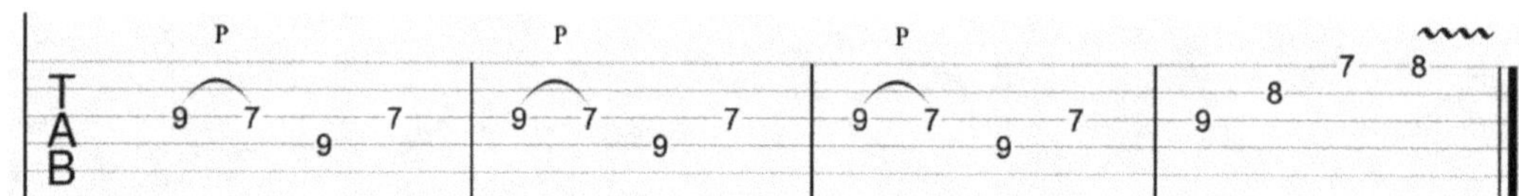

In this last example, you use a repeated lick, a pull-off, and end with vibrato.

Go through these examples, and work at creating your own. Also, work on mixing them for longer musical phrasing examples.

**Additional Melodic Contours in Lydian**

- **Emphasize the Raised Fourth:** Highlighting the raised fourth degree gives the Lydian mode its unique character.

Use this interval to create a sense of wonder and exploration in your melodies.

A Lydian:  A  B  C  D#  E  F#  G# = 1  2  3  #4  5  6  7

As you can see, in the A Lydian mode, the raised fourth note is the D#, so this is the note you want to emphasize.

Remember, the Lydian mode is a major, with a raised fourth. It is different from the Ionian mode.

- **Incorporate Wide Intervals:** The Lydian mode's structure allows for graceful leaps between notes.

Use wide intervals to craft melodies that feel expansive and uplifting.  Remember, an interval is the distance between notes. This is what you want to master within the modes.

- **Blend Dynamics and Articulation:** Vary your dynamics and articulation to enhance expressiveness. Smooth legato passages can convey a dreamy quality, while staccato notes add contrast and excitement.

This is where hammer-ons and pull-offs come into play.  Make sure to practice these techniques daily, as they are the foundation of melody.

- **Create Tension and Release:** Ascend to the raised fourth or the leading tone and resolve to the tonic or fifth for a satisfying melodic closure.

The raised fourth in Lydian sounds unstable and tends to move to the fifth, making it a strong leading tone.

- **Melody Transcription:** Listen to pieces using the Lydian mode and transcribe the melodies. This practice will enhance your ear and inspire new melodic ideas.

By mastering Lydian phrasing techniques, you'll be able to create melodies that capture the mode's distinctive qualities, enriching your musical expression and performance.

# Lesson 16:  Chords Within the Lydian Mode

The Lydian mode, known for its bright and ethereal sound, offers a distinctive set of chords that can add a touch of magic to your music.

Understanding the chords within the Lydian mode allows you to create harmonically rich compositions that highlight its unique character.

The Lydian mode is built on the fourth degree of the major scale and features a raised fourth. This gives it a sound that is both familiar and slightly otherworldly.

Each note in the Lydian scale can serve as the root of a chord, constructed by stacking thirds. Here's how the chords are constructed in the Lydian mode:

- **I (Tonic) -** Major Chord: The tonic chord is a major chord built on the first scale degree. It sets the bright, expansive tone of the mode. For example, in C Lydian, the tonic chord is C major (C-E-G).

C major:  C-w-D-w-E-h-F-w-G-w-A-w-B-h-Octave.

- **II (Supertonic)** - Major Chord: The supertonic chord is a major chord built on the second scale degree. It adds brightness and forward motion. In C Lydian, this is D major (D-Fsharp-A).

D major:  D-w-E-w-F#-h-G-w-A-w-B-w-C#-h-Octave.

- **iii (Mediant)** - Minor Chord: The mediant chord is a minor chord built on the third scale degree, providing a sense of contrast. In C Lydian, this is E minor (E-G-B)

E minor:  E-w-F#-h-G-w-A-w-B-h-C-w-D-w-Octave.

- **#iv (Raised Subdominant)** - Diminished Chord: The raised subdominant chord is a diminished chord, adding tension and intrigue. In C Lydian, this is F# diminished (F#-A-C).

Remember, when it comes to creating chords, it's all about knowing your notes.  The better you know your notes, the better you'll be at creating chords.

- **V (Dominant)** - Major Chord: The dominant chord is a major chord built on the fifth scale degree, creating tension that resolves back to the tonic. In C Lydian, this is G major (G-B-D).

G major:  G-w-A-w-B-h-C-w-D-w-E-w-F-h-Octave.

- **vi (Submediant)** - Minor Chord: The submediant chord is a minor chord built on the sixth scale degree, contributing to the mode's rich harmonic palette. In C Lydian, this is A minor (A-C-E).

A minor:  A-w-B-h-C-w-D-w-E-h-F-w-G-w-Octave.

- **vii (Leading Tone)** - Minor Chord: The leading tone chord is a minor chord built on the seventh scale degree, offering resolution to the tonic. In C Lydian, this is B minor (B-D-F#).

B minor:  B-w-C#-h-D-w-E-w-F#-h-G-w-A-w-Octave.

Experiment with different progressions to discover how these chords interact and enhance your compositions.

62

## Chapter IV Summary

<u>First</u>, you are introduced to the Lydian mode.  This is the fourth of the seven modes.  It is a major, similar to the Ionian mode, except it has a raised fourth, which gives it a bright, dreamy tone quality.

<u>Second</u>, you learn to transpose the mode just as you did with the others.  By playing this mode in different keys, you not only expand your roadmap of the fretboard, but also improve your knowledge of notes within different keys.

<u>Third</u>, you learn about Lydian mode phrasing.  Just like with the other three previously learned, you do this with hammer-ons, pull-offs, slides, and so forth.  This allows you to bring out the mode's characteristics.

<u>Fourth</u>, you learn about chords that can be created with the Lydian mode.  Since it is a major with a raised fourth, it provides chords different from those of the Phrygian, Dorian, and Ionian modes.  This allows you to enhance your chord vocabulary.

<u>Lastly</u>, the Lydian mode is the fourth of the seven.  A major with a raised fourth, giving it a different tone quality from the Ionian. Its formula is w-w-w-h-w-w-h, and like the others, should be committed to memory for best results.

# Chapter V:  The Mixolydian Mode

## Lesson 17:  Introduction to the Mixolydian Mode

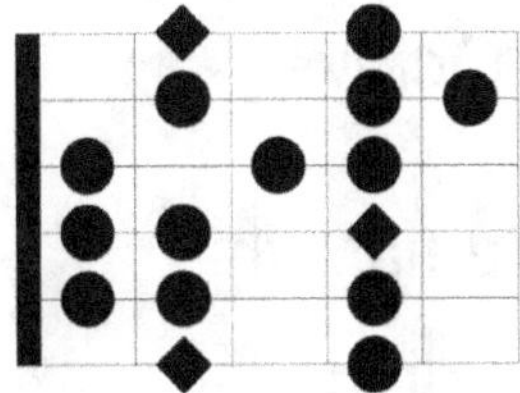

The Mixolydian mode is the fifth of the seven musical modes and is known for its distinctive, bluesy sound. It is similar to the major scale but features a lowered seventh degree, giving the mode a distinctive character.

### Understanding the Mixolydian Mode

- **Structure and Scale Degrees:** The Mixolydian mode consists of seven notes, labeled as degrees (I, II, III, IV, V, VI, VII).

The distinctive lowered seventh degree is a defining feature that distinguishes it from the Ionian mode and the major scale.

- **Tonic and Dominant Roles:** In the Mixolydian mode, the tonic serves as the home base, while the lowered seventh degree creates a characteristic tension that resolves to the tonic, offering a relaxed yet dynamic feel.

G Mixolydian:  G-w-A-w-B–h-C-w-D-w-E–h-F-w-Octave.

Remember, the Mixolydian mode is a major wth a flat 7th, making it a bit different from the Ionian and the Lydian.

Ionian mode:  1 2 3 4 5 6 7

Lydian mode:  1 2 3 #4 5 6 7

Mixolydian mode:  1 2 3 4 5 6 b7

## Characteristics of the Mixolydian Sound

A relaxed, slightly rebellious sound characterizes the Mixolydian mode. The lowered seventh degree creates tension that sets it apart from the traditional major scale, giving it a more laid-back, bluesy feel.

Its unique interval structure allows it to convey a wide range of emotions.

- **Emotional Qualities:** The Mixolydian mode's lowered seventh degree gives it a distinctive sound that can evoke a sense of relaxation and groove.

This makes it ideal for genres like blues, rock, and funk, where a smooth, soulful vibe is desired.

- **Common Usage:** The Mixolydian mode is frequently used in classic rock, blues, and jazz. Its adaptability makes it a favorite among musicians looking to add melodic interest and rhythmic drive to their compositions.

A Mixolydian:  A-w-B-w-C#-h-D-w-E-w-F#-h-G-w-Octave.

D Mixolydian:  D-w-E-w-F#-h-G-w-A-w-B-h-C-w-Octave.

- **Melodic and Harmonic Flexibility:** The Mixolydian mode's structure allows for fluid melodic lines and rich harmonic textures.

Its characteristic intervals provide a flexible foundation for crafting engaging melodies and dynamic chord progression.

## Common Applications of the Mixolydian Mode

- **Blues and Rock Music:** The Mixolydian mode is a staple in both genres due to its inherent bluesy quality.

The lowered seventh degree provides a natural fit for the dominant seventh chords typically used in these genres.

- **Jazz Improvisation:** In jazz, the Mixolydian mode is frequently used for improvisation over dominant seventh chords.

Jazz musicians appreciate the mode's ability to convey a relaxed yet complex sound, making it ideal for exploring intricate melodic ideas and harmonic variations.

By understanding the structure and characteristics of the Mixolydian mode, you'll gain valuable insights into its expressive potential and versatility.

This foundational knowledge will enhance your ability to create and perform music that resonates with depth and emotional richness.

## Lesson 18:  Mixolydian Mode in Different Keys

Transposing the Mixolydian mode is essential for developing your guitar versatility. By learning to play this mode in various keys, you can adapt its bluesy, relaxed sound to different musical contexts.

### Transposing the Mixolydian Mode

- **Identify the Root:** Determine the root note of the new key you wish to play in. For instance, if you're moving from G Mixolydian to D Mixolydian, D becomes your new root.

G Mixolydian:  G-w-A-w-B-h-C-w-D-w-E-h-F-w-Octave.

D Mixolydian:  D-w-E-w-F#-h-G-w-A-w-B-h-C-w-Octave.

- **Apply the Whole and Half Step Pattern:** Follow the Mixolydian mode's sequence of whole and half steps: whole, whole, half, whole, whole, half, whole. Start from your new tonic and apply this pattern to identify the notes of the scale in the new key.

- **Practice in Multiple Keys:** Regularly play the Mixolydian mode in different keys to familiarize yourself with the fretboard and enhance your adaptability.

This will allow you to switch keys fluidly during performances or improvisation sessions.

## Exercises for the Mixolydian Mode in Different Keys

To gain proficiency in playing the Mixolydian mode across different keys, it's important to incorporate specific exercises into your practice routine.  Just like with all the previous modes you've learned so far.

- **Key Transposition Exercise:** Choose a starting key and play the Mixolydian mode in that key. Shift to another key and play the mode again.

Continue this process through all 12 keys, focusing on maintaining accuracy and fluency throughout.

C Mixolydian:  C-w-D-w-E-h-F-wG-w-A-h-Bb-w-Octave.

E Mixolydian:  E-w-F#-w-G#-h-A-w-B-w-C#-h-D-w-Octave.

- **Fretboard Navigation Drills:** Just like with the other modes, select a key and play the Mixolydian mode in various positions along the fretboard.

This exercise will deepen your understanding of the neck and improve your ability to move seamlessly between keys.

B mixolydian: B-w-C#-w-D#-h-E-w-F#-w-G#-h-A-w-Octave.

F Mixolydian:  F-w-G-w-A-h-Bb-w-C-w-D-h-Eb-w-Octave.

- **Harmonization Practice:** In your chosen key, harmonize the Mixolydian mode by playing chords built on each scale degree.

This will enhance your understanding of how the mode's notes relate harmonically and improve your overall musicianship.

C Mixolydian:  C  D  E  F  G  A  B

C major:  C  E  G

D minor:  D  F  A

E  minor:  E  G  B

- **Work with Backing Tracks:** Use backing tracks in different keys and improvise using the Mixolydian mode. This exercise will develop your ear and improvisational skills, making you a more flexible and creative guitarist.

A Mixolydian:  A-w-B-w-C#-h-D-w-E-w-F#-h-G-w-Octave.

B Mixolydian:  B-w-C#-w-D#-h-E-w-F#-w-G#-h-A-w-Octave.

C Mixolydian:  C-w-D-w-E-h-F-w-G-w-A-h-Bb-w-Octave.

By mastering the Mixolydian mode across various keys, you'll expand your musical repertoire, gain confidence performing in diverse settings, and enrich your guitar playing and musical expression.

## Lesson 19:  Mixolydian Mode Phrasing

Developing effective phrasing in the Mixolydian mode can add a distinctive bluesy flavor to your playing. Like the other modes, we'll look at phrasing ideas for crafting expressive solos.

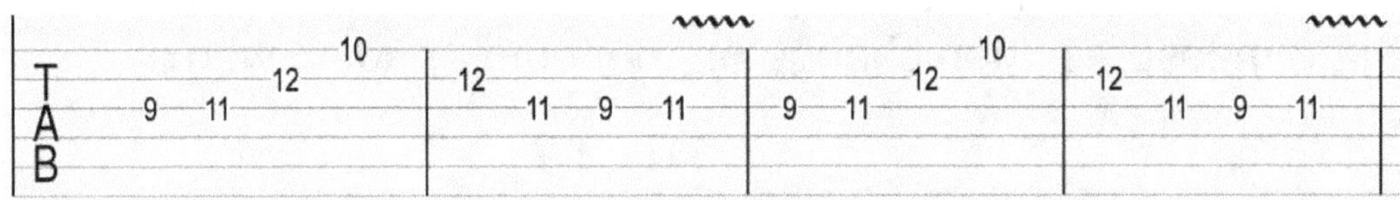

In this first phrasing example, you go through the mode with a two-measure phrase, ending it with vibrato.  Simple, yet effective as a repeated lick.

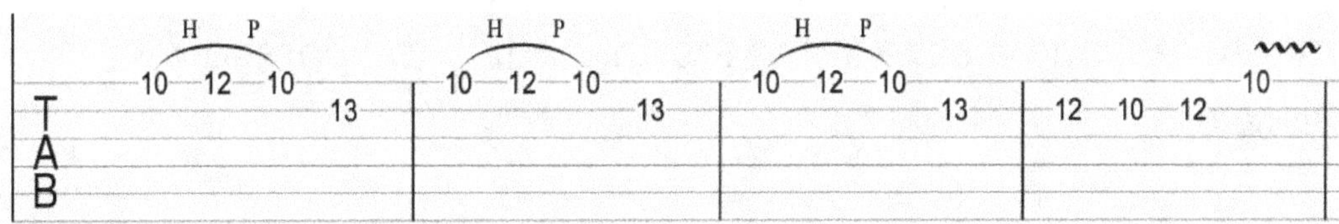

In this second example, you use the hammer-on pull-off technique for three measures, then vary it in the fourth measure.  Ending the phrase with vibrato.

72

Remember, vibrato is a great way to end a phrase, or anytime you want to add a pause.

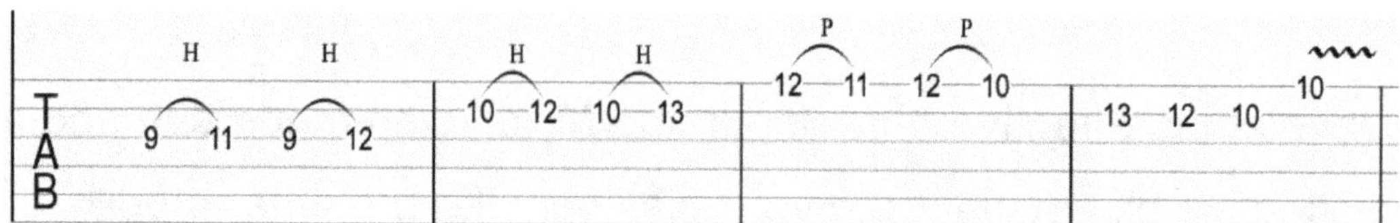

In this third example, you use hammer-ons and pull-offs over three measures, then change on the fourth, ending with a vibrato.

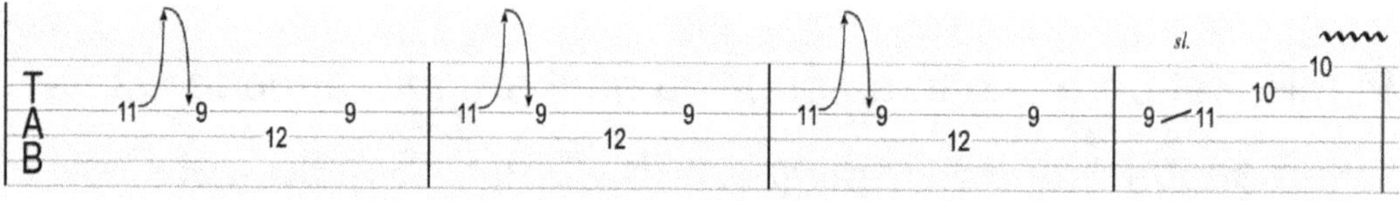

In this fourth example, you use a bend release over three measures, and a slide in the fourth, ending the phrase with a vibrato.

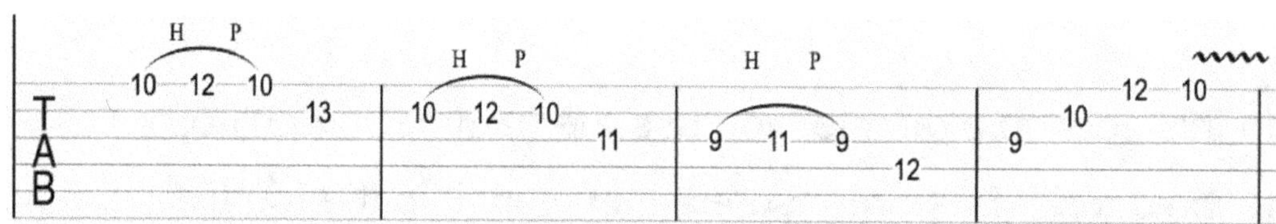

In this fifth example, you once again utilize a hammer-on pull-off over three measures, change on the fourth, and end with a vibrato.

## Additional Melodic Phrasing Ideas in Mixolydian

- **Emphasize the Lowered Seventh:** The Mixolydian mode is characterized by a lowered seventh. Highlight this note in your melodies to capture the mode's unique sound.

This can add a bluesy tension that resolves beautifully to the root, and since it has the lowered seventh note with a major 3rd, it works well with a dominant seventh chord built on the same interval.

- **Use Bluesy Bends and Slides:** Incorporate techniques like bends and slides to enhance the expressiveness of your phrases.

These elements are especially effective in the Mixolydian mode, where they can emphasize the mode's relaxed, soulful character.

Remember, the goal is to bring out the mode's characteristics. This can only be done by thoroughly understanding its note intervals and what makes it unique among the other six.

- **Incorporate Syncopation:** Add rhythmic interest by using syncopation in your phrasing. This can create a sense of movement and groove that resonates well with the Mixolydian's laid-back feel.

Common timing:  1  2  3  4 |  1  2  3  4 |  1 & 2 & 3 & 4 & |

Syncopated timing:  1  &  2  3  4 |  1  2  &  3  4 |  & 1  & 2  3  4 |

Notice how the syncopated timing has an odd cadence. Common time has a straightforward beat: 1, 2, 3, 4, whereas syncopated rhythms have an odd beat.

- **Odd Timing Catches Attention:** When you listen to syncopated rhythms, they stand out and are hard to replicate.  Make sure to experiment with this idea in your compositions.

By mastering these phrasing techniques, you'll be able to create compelling and expressive music in the Mixolydian mode, enriching your guitar playing and musical expression.

## Lesson 20:  Chords Within the Mixolydian Mode

The Mixolydian mode, with its distinctive lowered seventh degree, offers a rich palette for chord construction. Understanding the chords in the Mixolydian mode will enhance your ability to craft melodic landscapes.

### Constructing Chords in the Mixolydian Mode

The Mixolydian mode is built on the fifth degree of the major scale and is characterized by a lowered seventh. This gives it a sound that is both major and slightly modal, creating a relaxed, bluesy feel.

Just like all the other modes learned so far, each note in the Mixolydian scale can serve as the root of a chord, constructed by stacking thirds, which make up the foundation of all chords.

- **I (Tonic) -** Major Chord: The tonic chord is a major chord built on the first scale degree. It establishes the key and provides a sense of home. For example, in G Mixolydian, the tonic chord is G major (G-B-D).

Key of G major:  G-w-A-w-B-h-C-w-D-w-E-w-F#-h-Octave.

- **ii (Supertonic)** - Minor Chord: The supertonic chord is a minor chord built on the second scale degree, often used to add movement. In G Mixolydian, this is A minor (A-C-E).

Key of A minor: A-w-B-h-C-w-D-w-E-h-F-w-G-w-Octave.

- **iii (Mediant)** - Diminished Chord: The mediant chord is a diminished chord built on the third scale degree, adding tension and intrigue. In G Mixolydian, this is B diminished (B-D-F).

Remember, what makes the diminished is the flat fifth. In a diminished triad, you will have the flat 3rd and the flat 5th.

- **IV (Subdominant)** - Major Chord: The subdominant chord is a major chord built on the fourth scale degree, offering movement away from the tonic. In G Mixolydian, this is C major (C-E-G).

Key of C major:  C-w-D-w-E-h-F-w-g-w-A-w-B-h-Octave.

- **v (Dominant)** - Minor Chord: The dominant chord is a minor chord built on the fifth scale degree, providing a sense of tension that resolves back to the tonic. In G Mixolydian, this is D minor (D-F-A).

Key of D minor:  D-w-E-h-F-w-G-w-A-h-Bb-w-C-w-Octave.

- **vi (Submediant)** - Minor Chord: The submediant chord is a minor chord built on the sixth scale degree, contributing to the mode's unique harmonic flavor. In G Mixolydian, this is E minor (E-G-B).

Key of E minor:  E-w-F#-h-G-w-A-w-B-h-C-w-D-w-Octave.

- **bVII (Subtonic)** - Major Chord: The subtonic chord is a major chord built on the lowered seventh scale degree, adding a distinctive modal quality. In G Mixolydian, this is F major (F-A-C).

Key of F major:  F-w-G-w-A-h-Bb-w-C-w-D-w-E-h-Octave.

By mastering these chords and their functions within the Mixolydian mode, you can create music that is harmonically rich and emotionally resonant.

## Chapter V Summary

<u>First,</u> you learn about the fifth of the seven modes, the Mixolydian mode.  This mode is major and known for its distinct bluesy sound.  It is similar to the Ionian mode but features a lowered seventh degree.  Making it major with a slight twist.

<u>Second</u>, you learn how to play the mode in different keys. Transposing it just like the modes before it gives you a wider range along the fretboard.  By doing so, you develop a much better understanding of the Mixolydian mode.

<u>Third</u>, you learn about phrasing that you can create with the Mixolydian mode.  This will allow you to add a distinct bluesy flavor to your playing.  Remember, this is done with the techniques mentioned before.  Master these techniques.

<u>Fourth</u>, you learn about the chords that are found within the Mixolydian mode.  Once again, enabling you to enhance your knowledge of chord construction.  Just as with the other modes, each note can be the root of a chord.

<u>Lastly</u>, the Mixolydian mode is the fifth of the seven and found on the fifth tone degree within the key it's played in.  It is a major with a lowered seventh.  Giving it a different tone quality than the Ionian.  Its formula is w-w-h-w-w-h-w.

# Chapter VI:  The Aeolian Mode

## Lesson 21:  Introduction to the Aeolian Mode

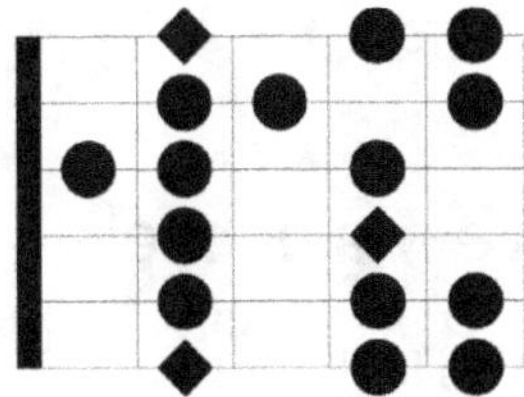

The Aeolian mode, also known as the natural minor scale, is one of the most widely used modes in music, loved for its emotive and introspective qualities.

It serves as a foundational scale for many genres, from classical to modern pop and rock.

Understanding the Aeolian Mode, characteristics of the Aeolian sound, and common applications of the Aeolian mode will allow you to compose compelling artistic music.

Its versatile structure supports fluid melodic lines and complex chord progressions, making it a powerful tool for composers and performers seeking to craft music that resonates with profound emotional richness.

## Understanding the Aeolian Mode

- **Scale Degrees and Structure:** The Aeolian mode consists of seven notes, labeled as degrees.  These degrees would be 1, 2, b3, 4, 5, b6, b7.  Also considered the natural minor mode.

It is constructed on the sixth degree of its relative major scale, with the minor third and minor seventh as key defining features of its sound.

G major:  G A B C D E F# Octave.
E Aeolian:  E F# G A B C D Octave = 6th tone degree.

- **Root and Dominant Roles:** In the Aeolian mode, the root serves as the home base, while the dominant provides tension that resolves back to the root.

This relationship is integral to the mode's harmonic movement and emotional expression.  Remember, the dominant is the 5th, which allows for the minor triad.

- **Sixth Tone Degree:**  Remember, the Aeolian mode can be located at the sixth tone degree of the major scale.

## Characteristics of the Aeolian Sound

The Aeolian mode is often described as melancholic, introspective, and haunting. Its unique interval structure allows it to convey a wide range of emotions, from sorrow and longing to introspective reflection.

- **Emotional Qualities:** The Aeolian mode's minor tonality lends it a somber, reflective quality that can evoke feelings of sadness, nostalgia, or introspection.

This makes it ideal for genres like blues, classical, and ballads, where emotional depth is desired.

- **Common Usage:** The Aeolian mode is widely used across musical genres, including classical, rock, pop, and jazz.

Its versatility enables musicians to craft melodies and harmonies that resonate with audiences across cultures and contexts.

- **Melodic and Harmonic Flexibility:** The Aeolian mode's structure supports fluid melodic lines and rich harmonic textures.

Its distinctive intervals provide a flexible foundation for creating expressive melodies and complex chord progressions.

## Applications of the Aeolian Mode

- **Classical Music:** Composers in the classical tradition often use the Aeolian mode to create pieces with depth and emotional resonance.

With its minor tonality, it is well-suited to conveying themes of tragedy and beauty simultaneously.

- **Rock and Pop Music:** In modern music, the Aeolian mode is a staple for crafting powerful ballads and introspective rock anthems.

By understanding the structure and characteristics of the Aeolian mode, you'll gain valuable insights into its expressive potential and versatility. Allowing you to compose compelling emotional music.

## Lesson 22:  The Aeolian Mode in Different Keys

Transposing the Aeolian mode across different keys is a valuable skill that enhances your versatility as a guitarist and helps you adapt to various musical contexts.

The Aeolian mode, known for its natural minor tonality, can be effectively utilized in multiple keys by understanding its structure and applying the appropriate steps.

### Transposing the Aeolian Mode

- **Identify the Root:** Determine the root note of the new key you want to transpose to. For example, if moving from A Aeolian to E Aeolian, E becomes your new tonic.

A Aeolian:  A-w-B-h-C-w-D-w-E-h-F-w-G-w-Octave.

E Aeolian:  E-w-F#-h-G-w-A-w-B-h-C-w-D-w-Octave.

- **Apply the Whole and Half Step Pattern:** Just like the other modes, the Aeolian mode follows a specific sequence of whole and half steps. Begin from your new root and apply this pattern to identify the scale notes.

C Aeolian:  C-w-D-h-Eb-w-F-w-G-Ab-h-Bb-w-Octave.

Remember, once you master the whole-step, half-step formula of the mode, you can find it in any key.

- **Practice in Multiple Keys:** Regularly practice the Aeolian mode in various keys to improve your familiarity with the fretboard and enhance your adaptability.

This will enable you to seamlessly incorporate the Aeolian sound into different musical settings and enhance your mastery of the fretboard.

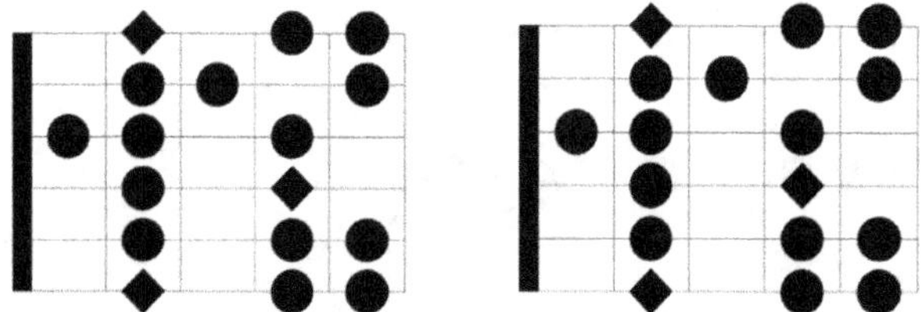

Play these at the 8th and 10th frets, and you would be playing C Aeolian and D Aeolian.  Now, determine the keys?

## Mastering Aeolian Mode in Different Keys

To become proficient in playing the Aeolian mode across multiple keys, incorporate the following exercises into your practice routine:

- **Key Transposition Exercise:** Choose a starting key and play the Aeolian mode. Shift to another key and play the mode again.

Continue this process through all 12 keys, focusing on accuracy and smooth transitions. Visualize the pattern to improve proficiency.

- **Work with Backing Tracks:** use them in various keys and improvise in Aeolian mode.

This exercise will develop your ear and improvisational skills, making you a more flexible and creative guitarist.

By mastering the Aeolian mode in different keys, you'll expand your musical repertoire and gain the confidence to perform effectively in diverse musical settings, enriching your overall guitar playing and musical expression.

## Lesson 23:  Aeolian Mode Phrasing

Crafting effective melodic phrases in the Aeolian mode requires understanding its melancholic, introspective qualities. Here are some phrasing examples to enhance your understanding of this evocative mode:

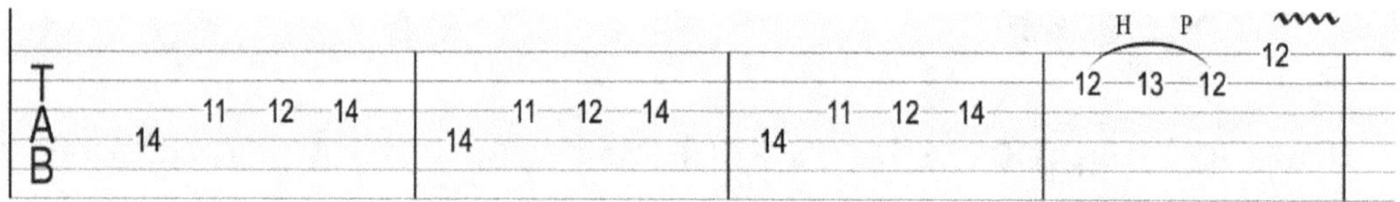

In this first phrasing example, you go through the mode with a repeated lick for three measures, then do a hammer-on pull-off and end the phrase with vibrato.

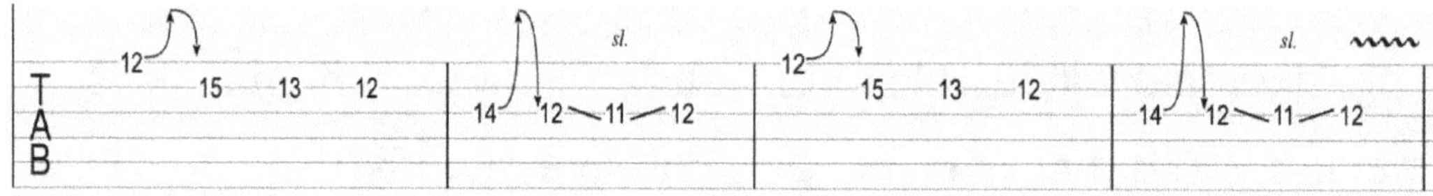

In this second example, start with a bend release, proceed through the mode with slides over two repeated measures, and end with vibrato.

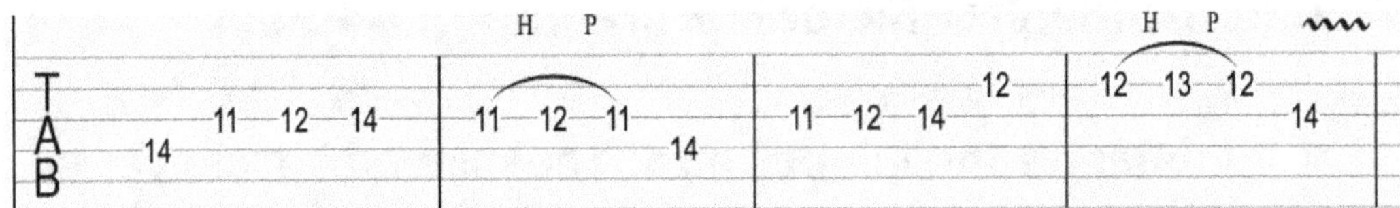

In this third phrasing example, you do another repeated lick that starts with a few notes, implements a hammer-on pull-off over two measures, and ends with vibrato.

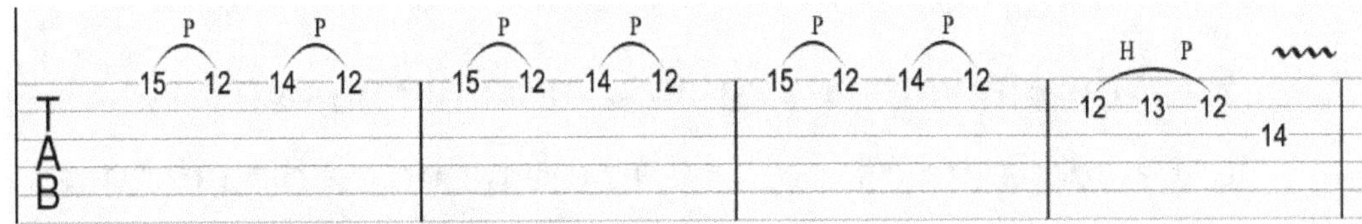

In the last example, you focus on pull-offs over three measures, and in the final one, you perform a hammer-on pull-off and end with a vibrato.

Once again, these phrasing examples utilize the hammer-on, pull-off, hammer-on pull-off, bends, slides, and vibrato—all techniques for crafting high-quality melodic musical landscapes.

Make sure to practice these techniques daily to develop muscle memory and get creative with making your own phrases.

## Additional Ides for Melodic Phrasing in Aeolian

- **Emphasize the Minor Third:** The minor third interval is crucial to the Aeolian mode's sound.

Use it to highlight the emotional depth and minor tonality, creating melodies that resonate with a sense of longing or introspection.

- **Experiment with Arpeggios:** Integrate arpeggios to underscore the minor triads in the mode, adding richness and complexity to your melodic lines.

This technique also helps reinforce the harmonic context of your melodies.  Understanding major and minor triads will enhance your ability to create diverse phrases.

By mastering these phrasing techniques, you'll be able to create memorable, emotionally resonant melodies in the Aeolian mode, enriching your musical expression and performance.

## Lesson 24: Chords Within the Aeolian Mode

The Aeolian mode is a staple in music for its emotive and introspective qualities. Understanding the chords within the Aeolian mode allows you to create rich, emotionally resonant music.

### Constructing Chords in the Aeolian Mode

The Aeolian mode is built on the sixth degree of the major scale and follows the pattern of whole and half steps: whole, half, whole, whole, half, whole, whole.

This pattern creates a naturally minor tonality. Here's how chords are constructed in the Aeolian mode:

**I (Tonic) -** Minor Chord: The tonic chord is a minor chord built on the first scale degree. It establishes the key and provides a sense of home. For example, in A Aeolian, the tonic chord is A minor (A-C-E).

A Aeolian:  A-w-B-h-C-w-D-w-E-h-F-w-G-w-Octave.

- **ii° (Supertonic) -** Diminished Chord: The supertonic chord is a diminished chord built on the second scale degree, adding tension and intrigue. In A Aeolian, this is B diminished (B-D-F).

*Remember, the diminished triad has a flat 3rd and 5th.

- **III (Mediant) -** Major Chord: The mediant chord is a major chord built on the third scale degree, offering brightness and contrast. In A Aeolian, this is C major (C-E-G).

C major:  C-w-D-w-E-h-F-w-G-w-A-w-B-h-Octave.

- **iv (Subdominant) -** Minor Chord: The subdominant chord is a minor chord built on the fourth scale degree, providing movement away from the tonic. In A Aeolian, this is D minor (D-F-A).

D minor:  D-w-E-h-F-w-G-w-A-h-Bb-w-C-w-Octave.

- **v (Dominant) -** Minor Chord: The dominant chord is a minor chord built on the fifth scale degree, creating tension that resolves back to the tonic. In A Aeolian, this is E minor (E-G-B).

E minor:  E-w-F#-h-G-w-A-w-B-h-C-w-D-w-Octave.

- **VI (Submediant) -** Major Chord: The submediant chord is a major chord built on the sixth scale degree, frequently used in progressions to evoke emotion. In A Aeolian, this is F major (F-A-C).

F major:  F-w-G-w-A-h-Bb-w-C-w-D-w-E-h-Octave.

**VII (Subtonic) -** Major Chord: The subtonic chord is a major chord built on the seventh scale degree, offering a strong resolution back to the tonic. In A Aeolian, this is G major (G-B-D).

G major:  G-w-A-w-B-h-C-w-D-w-E-w-F#-h-Octave.

By mastering these chords and their functions within the Aeolian mode, you can create music that is harmonically rich and emotionally resonant.

92

## Chapter VI Summary

<u>First</u>, you learn about the Aeolian mode.  This is the sixth of the seven modes, and is otherwise known as the natural minor.  This mode has a lowered third, sixth, and seventh, producing a sad, somber sound.

<u>Second</u>, you learn how to transpose it into different keys.  Just like with the other modes, this will enhance your knowledge of the fretboard.  It will also expand the fretboard roadmap when connected to the other five, enhancing your musicianship.

<u>Third</u>, you learn about phrasing examples that can be used with the Aeolian mode.  Just like the others, this will let you bring out the mode's character.  Make sure to work on your phrasing techniques to make this happen.

<u>Fourth</u>, you learn about chords that can be found inside the Aeolian mode.  Since it is a minor mode, you start with a minor chord.  By going through the notes and figuring out the chords, you add to your chord vocabulary.

<u>Lastly</u>, the Aeolian mode is the natural minor, the sixth of the seven modes, and can be found at the 6th tone degree of the major scale.  Its formula is w-h-w-w-h-w-w.  Master this note interval to get the best out ofthe Aeolian mode.

# Chapter VII: The Locrian Mode

## Lesson 25: Introduction to the Locrian

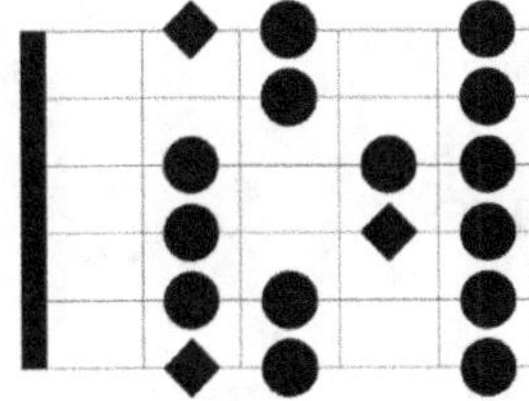

The Locrian mode is the seventh and final mode of the diatonic scale family and is perhaps the most distinctive. This is because the Locrian mode is characterized by a diminished fifth, which gives it a unique, unstable quality.

**Understanding the Locrian Mode**

The Locrian mode is formed by starting on the seventh degree of the major scale and follows a distinct pattern of whole and half steps: half, whole, whole, half, whole, whole, whole.

This sequence creates a diminished fifth interval, a hallmark of the Locrian mode and a contributor to its inherently unstable sound.

- **Scale Degrees and Structure:** The Locrian mode consists of seven notes, labeled as degrees (I, II, III, IV, V, VI, VII).

It is based on the seventh degree of the major scale, with the diminished fifth as a defining interval that distinguishes it from other modes.

G major:  G-w-A-w-B-h-C-w-D-w-E-w-F#-h-Octave.

Fsharp Locrian:  F#-h-G-w-A-w-B-h-C-w-D-w-E-w-Octave.

Notice how F sharp is the 7th of G major.  This is where the F sharp Lorian mode begins and remains the same throughout. Notice how they are the same as G major, but in a different order.

Starting on F sharp instead of G produces a different color because the whole-step/half-step formula changes.

- **Root and Dominant Roles:** In the Locrian mode, the tonic serves as the starting point, but the diminished fifth prevents the strong sense of resolution typically found in other modes. This lack of resolution creates tension.

## Characteristics of the Locrian Sound

The Locrian mode is distinguished by its dissonant and unresolved nature, primarily due to the diminished fifth interval. This gives it a sense of instability that can evoke tension and unease, making it less common as a choice for traditional melodies and chord progressions.

- **Common Usage:** While the Locrian mode is not frequently used in mainstream music, it appears in niche genres and specific musical contexts that embrace its unconventional sound.

Composers and musicians who enjoy pushing the boundaries of traditional harmony may find the Locrian mode a valuable addition to their creative toolkit.

Understanding the Locrian mode's characteristics will help you incorporate its unique sound into your guitar playing and songwriting. Giving you opportunities to experiment with more complex and unconventional musical ideas.

## Lesson 26:  Locrian Mode in Different Keys

Transposing the Locrian mode to different keys enhances your versatility as a guitarist and broadens your musical palette. This lesson focuses on transposition and includes exercises to help you master the Locrian mode across various keys.

### Transposing the Locrian Mode

Understanding how to transpose the Locrian mode requires familiarity with its unique interval structure.

**Identify the tonic:** Determine the root note of the key you wish to transpose to. For example, if you're moving from B Locrian to F Locrian, F becomes your new tonic.

B Locrian:  B-h-C-w-D-w-E-h-F-w-G-w-A-w-Octave.

F Locrian:  F-h-Gb-w-Ab-w-Bb-h-Cb-w-Db-w-Eb-w-Octave.

Notice how the notes in these two modes change, but the whole step formula stays the same.  The Locrian mode (as well as all the others) will always have the same scientific formula.

This is what you want to master when it comes to the modes when moving them around the fretboard.

- **Practice in Multiple Keys:** Regularly practice the Locrian mode in different keys to improve your familiarity with the fretboard.

This will enable you to adapt the mode to various musical contexts, despite its inherent tension.

- **Apply the Interval Pattern:** Use the Locrian mode's sequence of whole and half steps: half, whole, whole, half, whole, whole, whole.

Start with your new root and follow this pattern to determine the scale's notes in the new key.  Listen for the mode's character to shine through as you play it.

## Mastering Locrian Mode in Different Keys

To become proficient in playing the Locrian mode across multiple keys, incorporate the following exercises into your practice routine:

- **Key Transposition Exercise:** Select a starting key and play the Locrian mode in that key. Shift to another key and play the mode again.

Continue this process through all 12 keys, focusing on accuracy and fluency, enhancing your mastery of the fretboard.

- **Fretboard Navigation Drill:** Choose a key and play the Locrian mode in different positions along the fretboard.

As stated before, this will deepen your understanding and improve your ability to move effortlessly between keys.

Make sure to practice visualization, as it will help you imprint the mode pattern in your mind for easier learning.

- **Harmonization Practice:** In your chosen key, harmonize the Locrian mode by playing chords built on each scale degree.

This will help you understand how the mode's notes relate harmonically, despite its complex tonal landscape.

- **Work with Backing Tracks:** Use backing tracks in various keys and explore the Locrian mode. As you go through the mode, listen to how the notes work with the chord progression.

This exercise will develop your ear and guitar skills, enabling you to explore the mode's enigmatic, tension-filled sound.

- **Certain Musical Contexts:** The Locrian mode is effective only in certain musical contexts. If you have issues working with it to ensure it sounds correct, study it further.

Remember, the Locrian mode has a dark, moody sound due to its flat fifth, and although it may not work well with conventional genres like pop, it can work well in styles like heavy metal.

By mastering the Locrian mode across different keys, you'll expand your musical repertoire, gain confidence performing in diverse settings, and enhance your overall guitar playing and musical expression.

100

## Lesson 27:  Locrian Mode Phrasing

The Locrian mode, known for its distinctive diminished fifth,
offers a unique and challenging platform for melodic phrasing.
The reason is the unresolved tension it creates.

As before with the other modes, we will explore phrasing
examples that will work for crafting expressive phrases within
the Locrian mode and integrating them into your playing.

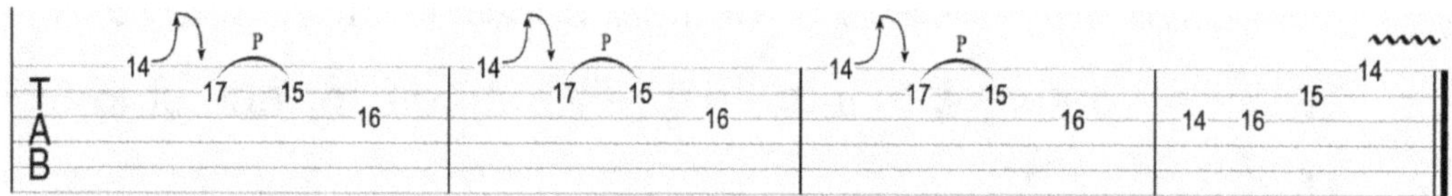

In this first phrasing example, you utilize a bend release, a
pull-off, and a repeated lick with a variation in measure four and
vibrato at the end.

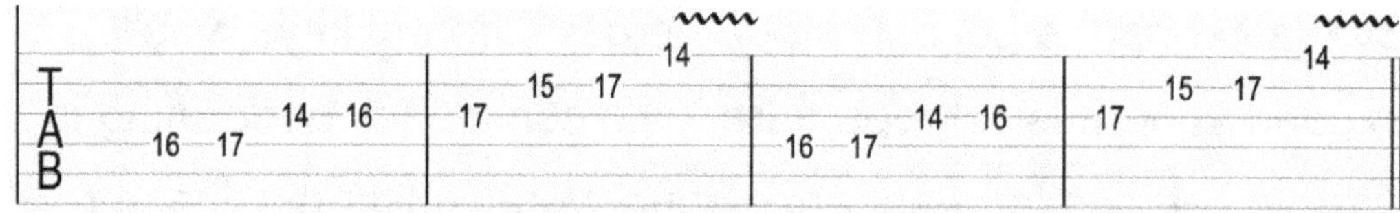

This second example uses a simple run-through of the mode in
two measures, repeated, and ends with vibrato in the fourth.

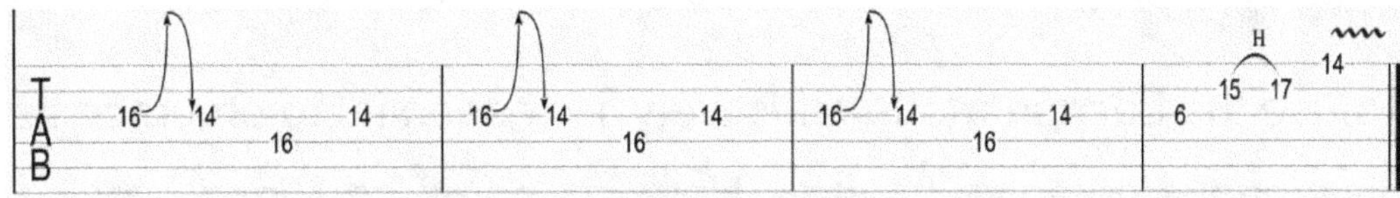

In this third phrasing example, you utilize a bend release, a hammer-on, and vibrato.  Done with a repeated lick over three measures and changed on the fourth.

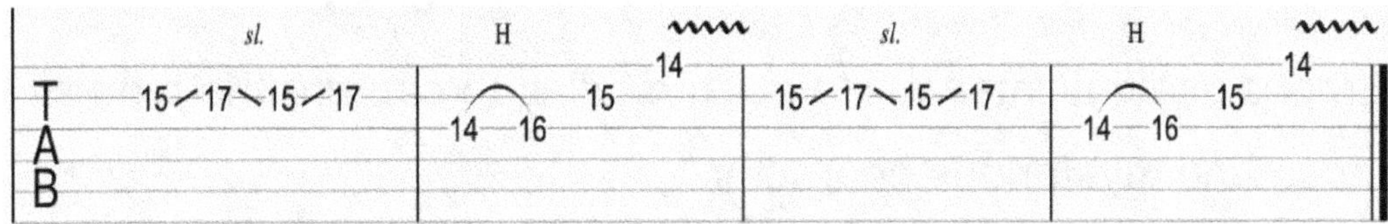

In this fourth example, you start with sliding up and down, use a hammer-on, and end with a vibrato.  Use a repeated lick over two measures.

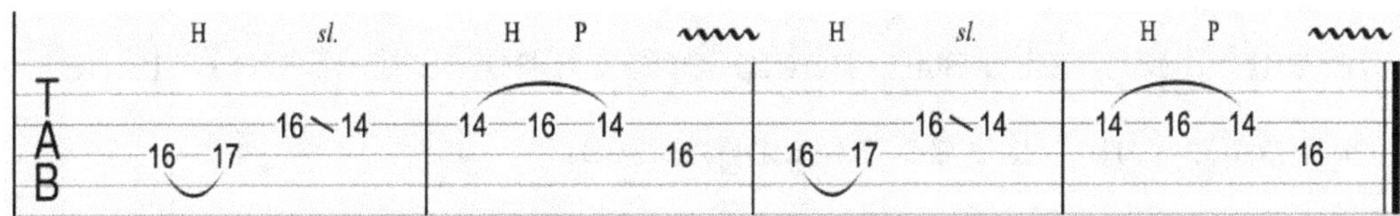

In this last example, you start with a hammer-on, proceed with a slide down, execute a hammer-on pull-off, and end the phrase with vibrato.  Repeat this over two measures.

Remember, work on these daily for the best results.

## Additional Ideas For Crafting Phrases in Locrian

To use the Locrian mode effectively, it's essential to embrace its dissonant, unresolved nature. Here are some additional ideas to help you create compelling melodic phrases.

- **Highlight the Diminished Fifth:** It is central to the Locrian mode's sound.

Emphasize this interval in your melodies to capture the mode's tense and mysterious character.

- **Use Chromatic Movement:** Incorporate chromatic passages to add tension and complexity to your phrases.

This can enhance the mode's dissonant quality and create interest. Just make sure not to land on notes that are outside the mode. Only use as passing tones.

- **Experiment with Unresolved Tension:** Allow some phrases to remain unresolved, reflecting the inherent instability of the Locrian mode.

This is what makes this mode unique from the others. It can evoke suspense and intrigue within the melody.

## Lesson 28:  Chords Within the Locrian Mode

The Locrian mode, known for its distinctive diminished fifth, features a unique set of chords that give it an enigmatic, tense sound.

Understanding the chords in the Locrian mode enables you to explore its complex harmonic landscapes.

### Constructing Chords in the Locrian Mode

The Locrian mode is built on the seventh degree of the major scale and is characterized by a flat fifth. This gives the mode its signature, unstable, dissonant quality.

- **I (Tonic)** - Diminished Chord: The tonic chord is a diminished chord built on the first scale degree. It sets the tense, unresolved tone of the mode. For example, in B Locrian, the tonic chord is B diminished (B-D-F).

Remember, the diminished will have the flat third and the flat fifth.  B-D-F = 1  b3, b5.  This goes with all diminished triads. Making them unique from the minor.

- **ii° (Supertonic)** - Diminished Chord: The supertonic chord is also a diminished chord built on the second scale degree, reinforcing the mode's dissonant character. In B Locrian, this is C diminished (C-Eb-Gb).

Once again, the chord is utilizing the flat third and the flat fifth.

- **III (Mediant)** - Major Chord: The mediant chord is a major chord built on the third scale degree, providing a brief moment of brightness. In B Locrian, this is Db major (Db-F-Ab).

D flat major:  Db-w-Eb-w-F-h-Gb-w-Ab-w-Bb-w-C-h-Octave.

- **iv (Subdominant)** - Minor Chord: The subdominant chord is a minor chord built on the fourth scale degree, adding a touch of melancholy. In B Locrian, this is Eb minor (Eb-Gb-Bb).

E flat minor:  Eb-w-F-h-Gb-w-Ab-w-Bb-h-Cb-w-Db-w-Octave.

Remember to master the whole-step formula across the major, minor, and diminished keys.  This will help you to master the modes and the chords within them.

- **v° (Dominant) -** Diminished Chord: The dominant chord is a diminished chord built on the fifth scale degree, creating tension that seeks resolution. In B Locrian, this is F diminished (F-Ab-Cb).

F diminished will once again utilize the 1, b3, and b5.

- **VI (Submediant) -** Major Chord: The submediant chord is a major chord built on the sixth scale degree, offering a contrast to the mode's overall dissonance. In B Locrian, this is G flat major (Gb-Bb-Db).

G major:  G-w-A-w-B-h-C-w-D-w-E-w-F#-h-Octave.

- **VII (Subtonic) -** Minor Chord: The subtonic chord is a minor chord built on the seventh scale degree, adding depth to the harmonic palette. In B Locrian, this is Ab minor (Ab-Cb-Eb).

A flat minor:  Ab-w-Bb-h-Cb-w-Db-w-Eb-h-Fb-w-Gb-w-Octave.

Experiment with different progressions to discover how these chords interact and enhance your compositions.

## Chapter VII Summary

First, you learn about the Locrian mode.  The final of the seven, and a very unique mode, as it is diminished by the lowered fifth. This mode has a very unresolved sound, so it is not used in most popular music.

Second, you learn how to transpose the mode into different keys.  Like the other six modes, this allows you to expand your fretboard roadmap and get more familiar with the mode itself. Allowing you to enhance your musicianship.

Third, you learn about phrasing with the Locrian mode.  This enables you to explore the mode in depth and determine whether and where it might fit into your compositions. Remember to practice your phrasing techniques daily.

Fourth, you learn about chords within the mode.  Since this is a diminished mode, it will start with a diminished triad.  A triad is a three-note chord, and the foundation for all chords to build on. Make sure to master the triad formulas.

Lastly, the Locrian mode is the seventh mode, because of the lowered fifth, it is diminished.  Because of this, the mode has an unresolved tone and can work within certain musical contexts. The formula is h-w-w-h-w-w-w.  Master this formula.

# Chapter VIII: Additional Concepts

## Lesson 29: Mixing the Modes

Mixing the modes is an exciting technique that adds complexity and depth to your music. By transitioning between different modes within a piece, you can create dynamic contrasts and evoke a wider range of emotions.

### Techniques for Transitioning Between Modes

When mixing modes, smooth transitions are crucial to maintain the flow and coherence of your music. Here are some techniques to help you transition seamlessly between modes:

- **Pivot Tones:** Use common notes between two modes as pivot tones to facilitate a smooth transition.

For example, if transitioning from the Ionian mode to the Dorian mode, use the common root note to pivot between the two.

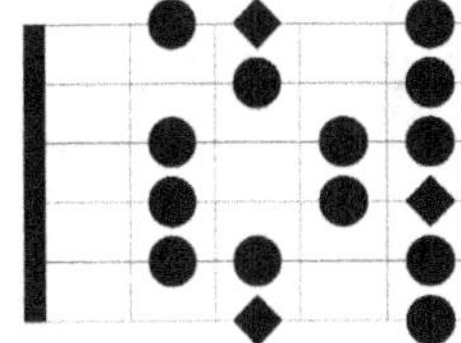 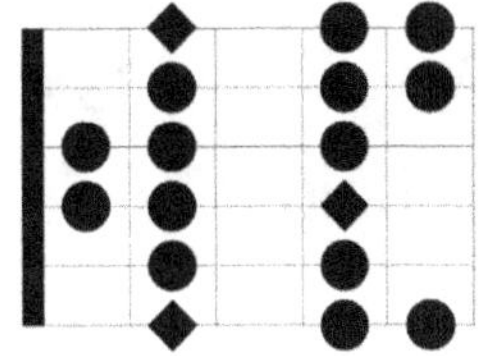

- **Shared Chords:** Identify chords that are shared between modes and use them as a bridge.

For instance, the I chord in the Ionian mode can act as a pivot when transitioning to the Lydian mode.

G major in Ionian:  G  B  D
C major in Lydian:  C  E  G

- **Modulation Techniques:** Apply modulation techniques such as key changes to introduce a new mode.

This can be done by modifying a chord progression to naturally lead into the new mode's tonal center.

Key of A minor:  A  B  C  D  E  F  G  Octave.

Key of C major:  C  D  E  F  G  A  B  Octave.

- **Melodic Motifs:** Develop a melodic motif that can be slightly altered to fit both modes. This creates a thematic link and eases the listener into the transition.

Since C major and A minor work well together, this would be a great place to execute this technique.

- **Gradual Shifts:** Transition gradually by introducing elements of the new mode while still playing within the original mode. This allows the listener to acclimate to the new tonal landscape.

Remember, because all modes share the same key, they contain the same notes, which is where this concept comes in handy.

## Benefits of Mode Mixing

- **Emotional Range:** By exploring different modes, you can evoke a broader spectrum of emotions, from the uplifting energy of Ionian to the introspective mood of Aeolian.

The Ionian mode is major, and the Aeolian mode is minor. Using these two modes in the same key adds contrast to your emotional landscape.

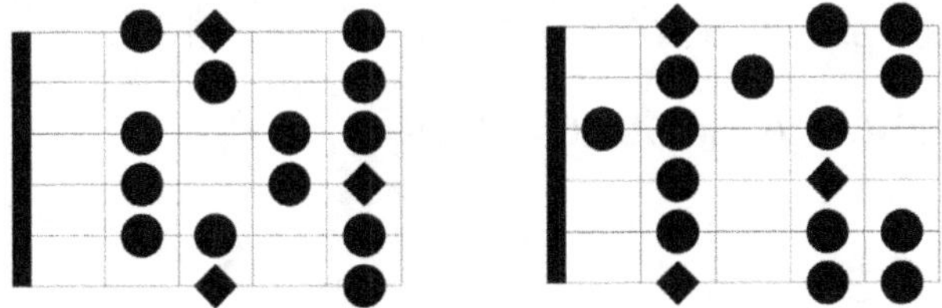

Work on going back and forth between these two modes.

- **Musical Interest:** Mode mixing adds variety and complexity, keeping your compositions engaging and preventing them from becoming monotonous.

This also allows you to enhance your knowledge of each individual mode, as well as unlock the mysteries of the fretboard.

- **Expressive Freedom:** Transitioning between modes allows greater improvisational freedom, enabling you to express nuanced emotions and ideas.

Once again, allowing you to enhance your ability to move around the fretboard and master key modulation.

- **Innovative Compositions:** By combining modes, you can create unique musical textures and structures, distinguishing your work from others.

This is the beauty of the half steps in the modes: they offer a wide range of ideas to enhance your songwriting.

- **Enhanced Creativity:** Experimenting with mode mixing encourages creative thinking and exploration, pushing the boundaries of traditional music theory.  This is where the lesson on phrasing comes in.

By mastering these concepts to the point where you can create your own, you will expand your creativity to the point of exploring uncharted territory.  This is where true innovation exists.

- **Mixing Modes:** You unlock a world of possibilities for creative musical expression.

As you get more familiar with each mode, you train your ear to hear notes better, and you master locations along the fretboard.

Enabling you to craft compositions that are rich, dynamic, and emotionally resonant.

Remember,  all these concepts require daily study and practice. If you put in the time and effort, your playing will reach a whole new level.

## Lesson 30:  Improvising with the Modes

Improvisation is a vital skill for any musician, allowing you to express yourself freely and adapt to different musical contexts. Mastering improvisation with modes can elevate your playing and open up new avenues for creativity.

This lesson will guide you through developing improvisational skills using modes and demonstrate how to incorporate them into live performances.

### Developing Improvisational Skills

Improvisation is about spontaneity and expression, but it also requires a strong foundation in technique and theory. Here are some steps to enhance your improvisational skills using modes:

- **Familiarize Yourself with Each Mode:** Practice each mode individually, focusing on its unique sound and character. This will help you recognize and utilize the specific tonal qualities of each mode during improvisation.

- **Learn Modal Patterns:** Practice common modal patterns and phrases that you can use as building blocks in your solos.

Having a repertoire of patterns will give you a foundation to draw from when improvising.

- **Explore Modal Intervals:** Experiment with the intervals that define each mode, such as the raised fourth in Lydian or the lowered seventh in Mixolydian.

Use these intervals to create interesting melodic lines. This will enhance your ability to utilize the unique character of each.

- **Practice with Backing Tracks:** Backing tracks are an excellent way to improve your improvisation. They provide a foundation to build on.

Remember, this is like going into no man's land, and helping you to develop your ear and adapt your playing to various musical situations.

- **Record and Review:** Record your improvisation sessions and listen to them later. By doing so, you identify areas where you excel and areas where improvement is needed.

This allows you to reflect on your practice sessions and enhances your growth and technical proficiency.

## Using Modes in Live Performances

Incorporating modes into live performances can add depth and variety to your music. Here are some strategies for using modes effectively on stage:

- **Set the Mood:** Choose modes that match the emotional tone you want to convey. For example, use the Dorian mode for a soulful, introspective piece, or the Mixolydian mode for a lively, bluesy feel.

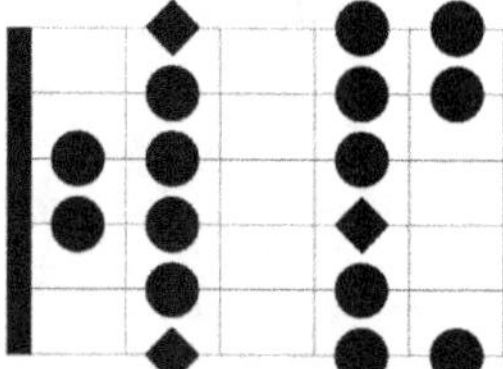 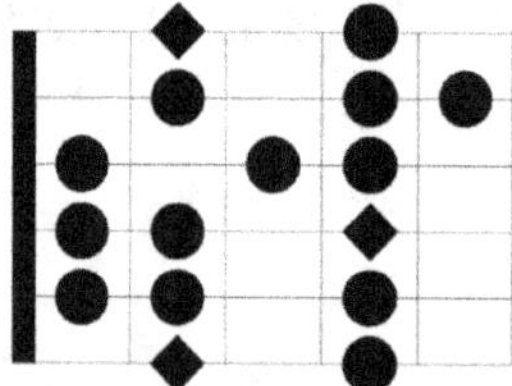

- **Build Dynamic Solos:** Use different modes to create contrast within your solos. Start with a mode that sets a specific tone, such as Phrygian, then transition to another, such as Aeolian, to add excitement or tension.

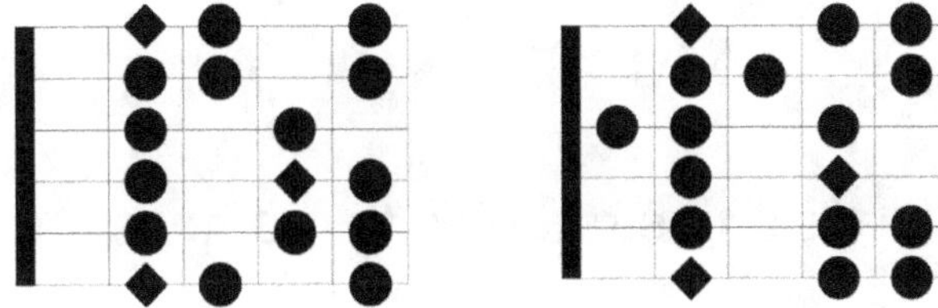

- **Interact with the Band:** Pay attention to what your fellow musicians are playing and use modes to complement their parts.

This interaction can create cohesive, engaging elements of the song that stand out and capture the audience's attention.

By developing your improvisational skills and learning to use modes effectively in live performances, you can become a more versatile and expressive musician.

## Lesson 31:  Composing with the Modes

Using different modes can add richness and variety to your music. As you know, each mode offers a distinct character and emotional palette.  Enabling you to craft pieces that resonate with listeners in different ways.

In this lesson, we'll explore ideas and strategies for composing with modes and for enhancing your songs by incorporating mode variations.

## Compositional Strategies

- **Identify the Mood and Emotion:** Begin by deciding the mood or emotion you want to convey in your composition. Each mode has its own emotional quality.

The Ionian is bright and joyful, the Dorian is soulful, the Phrygian is exotic, the Lydian is mystical, and the Mixolydian is relaxed and bluesy.

The Aeolian is somber and introspective, and the Locrian is tense and mysterious. Choose a mode that best fits the desired mood.

- **Create a Modal Framework:** Establish a clear modal framework for your composition by selecting a key and identifying the mode.

Use the mode's characteristic notes and intervals to build melodies and harmonies that reflect its unique sound.

- **Develop a Motif:** Craft a motif that highlights the distinctive intervals of the chosen mode.

A strong motif can serve as the foundation of your composition, providing thematic cohesion and a recognizable hook for listeners.

- **Use Modal Chord Progressions:** Incorporate chord progressions that emphasize the mode's unique qualities. Experiment with both traditional and unconventional progressions.

By doing so, you can create harmonic interest and tension within your compositions that is attractive to the listener.

## Enhancing Songs with Mode Variation

- **Mode Shifting:** Introduce mode shifts within a composition to create contrast and maintain listener interest.

Transition smoothly between modes using shared notes or chords to ensure cohesion.

- **Contrast Sections:** Use different modes in contrasting sections of your composition, such as verses and choruses, to highlight their emotional differences.

For example, use the Aeolian mode for a melancholic verse and then switch to the Ionian mode for an uplifting chorus.

- **Layer Modal Textures:** Experiment with layering different modes across instruments. For instance, have one instrument play a melody in Phrygian while another provides harmonic support in Dorian.

By employing these strategies and techniques, you can effectively use modes to compose music that is expressive, engaging, and memorable.

## Lesson 32:  Ear Training With the Modes

Developing a strong ear is essential for mastering guitar modes and enhancing your overall musicianship. Ear training helps you recognize modes by sound, identify intervals, and improve your improvisational skills.

In this lesson, we'll explore two key topics: Recognizing Modes by Ear and Interval Identification.

### Recognizing Modes by Ear

Recognizing different modes by ear is a valuable skill that lets you quickly identify a piece of music's mode and respond accordingly. Here's how you can develop this ability:

- **Listen Actively:** Spend time listening to music that prominently features different modes.

Pay attention to the unique qualities of each mode, such as the bright, uplifting sound of the Ionian or the exotic, mysterious feel of the Phrygian.

- **Mode Identification Exercise:** Use recordings or create your own progressions in various modes. Play them back and try to identify the mode by ear.

Start with intervals and gradually increase the complexity to include entire progressions.

- **Sing the Modes:** Singing the notes of each mode helps internalize their sound. Sing along with a scale or a melody in a chosen mode.

Focus on its characteristic intervals. This practice can reinforce your auditory memory of each mode.

- **Compare and Contrast:** Listen to two different modes back-to-back and note their differences. For example, compare Lydian and Ionian; focus on the raised fourth in Lydian.

Remember, these two modes are similar except for the raised fourth in Lydian.  This contrast can help sharpen your mode recognition skills.

## Interval Identification

Intervals are the building blocks of modes and melodies. Training your ear to recognize intervals will enhance your ability to play by ear and improvise. Here are some tips on how to develop this skill:

- **Interval Recognition Drills:** Practice identifying intervals by ear. Start with simple intervals, such as major and minor seconds.

Gradually work your way up to more complex ones, such as perfect fourths and tritones.

- **Use Reference Songs:** Associate specific intervals with familiar songs or melodies.

For example, the opening of "Here Comes the Bride" is a perfect fourth. This technique can help recall intervals more easily.

Remember, the more you work on this concept, the easier it will be to play and write songs.

- **Interactive Apps and Tools:** Use ear-training apps or online tools designed for interval recognition.

These resources provide exercises and quizzes to help you test and improve your skills.

With all the resources that you have available today, there is no reason you can't master these concepts.

- **The Digital Age:** We now live in a world that makes these techniques and concepts easier than ever to master, in half the amount of time.

By focusing on recognizing modes by ear and identifying intervals, you'll enhance your ability to understand and interpret music more intuitively.

These ear training skills will not only improve your improvisation and composition but also deepen your appreciation and enjoyment of music.

## Lesson 33:  Effective Practice Habits

Developing effective practice habits is essential for mastering the guitar and improving your overall musicianship. By establishing a structured practice routine, you can optimize your learning process and maintain motivation.

Let's look at ways to set up a productive practice schedule and strategies for tracking your progress to achieve your musical goals.

### Setting a Practice Routine

Creating a consistent practice routine is the cornerstone of effective learning. Here are some steps to help you establish a routine that works for you:

- **Set Clear Goals:** Define what you want to achieve in each practice session. Whether it's mastering a specific mode, improving your improvisation skills, or composing with modes, having clear objectives will keep you focused and motivated.

- **Allocate Time Wisely:** Decide how much time you can dedicate to practice each day.

Consistency is key, so aim for shorter, focused sessions rather than infrequent, lengthy ones. Even 20-30 minutes of daily practice can yield significant results.

- **Balance Your Practice:** Divide your practice time among different activities, such as scales, improvisation, and composition.

This variety will keep your sessions engaging and ensure that you develop well-rounded skills.

- **Warm Up Properly:** Begin each session with a warm-up routine that includes finger exercises and basic scales.

This process prepares your hands for playing and develops finger dexterity and independence, reducing the risk of injury.

- **Focus on Technique:** Dedicate part of your session to honing your technique, including finger placement, picking accuracy, and timing. Mastery of technique will enhance your ability to express yourself musically.

## Tracking Your Progress

Monitoring your progress is crucial for staying motivated and identifying areas for improvement. Here's how you can effectively track your musical journey:

- **Keep a Practice Journal:** Record your goals, accomplishments, and challenges.

Reflecting on your practice sessions will help you identify patterns and areas that need attention.

- **Record Your Playing:** Regularly record your practice sessions and listen back to evaluate your progress.

Audio or video recordings provide valuable feedback on your technique, timing, and musicality.

By establishing effective practice habits and diligently tracking your progress, you'll build a strong foundation for mastering guitar modes and enhancing your overall musicianship.

Embrace the journey of learning and enjoy the satisfaction that comes with each new achievement.

## Chapter VIII Summary

<u>First</u>, you learn how mixing modes can be an effective technique that adds complexity and depth to your music.  By transitioning between different modes within a piece, you can create dynamic contrasts and evoke a wider range of emotions.

<u>Second</u>, you learn about improvising.  This is a vital skill for any guitarist, allowing you to express yourself freely and adapt to different musical contexts. This can elevate your playing and open up new avenues for creativity.

<u>Third</u>, you learn to compose using the modes.  As you know, each mode offers a distinct character and emotional palette. This enables you to craft pieces that resonate with listeners in different ways.

<u>Fourth</u>, you learn how the modes can support ear training.  A strong ear is essential for mastering guitar modes and enhancing your overall musicianship. Ear training helps you recognize modes by sound and identify intervals.

<u>Lastly</u>, you learn how to develop effective practice habits. These are essential for optimized progress.  By establishing a structured practice routine, you can optimize your learning process and maintain motivation.

# Guitar Mode Mastery: Conclusion

As we reach the end of the "Beginner's Guide to Guitar Mode Mastery," it's time to reflect on the journey you've undertaken. This guide has equipped you with a comprehensive understanding of the seven modes.

From the bright and uplifting Ionian mode to the mysterious and tension-filled Locrian mode, you have explored the depth and diversity that these musical scales offer. Adding a rich array of tools to your musical toolkit

Throughout this guide, you've encountered practical exercises to help solidify your understanding and application of each mode. Whether through transposing modes to different keys, or developing melodic phrasing.

Remember that practice is key to mastering these concepts, and consistent, focused practice will continue to deepen your understanding and proficiency. As well as boost your confidence.

In addition to technical skills, this journey has encouraged you to explore the emotional and expressive potential of each mode.  Music is a language of emotion, and understanding how different modes can convey an array of musical expression.

These insights not only enhance your playing and fretboard knowledge but also enrich your overall musical experience, allowing you to connect more deeply with your audience and fellow musicians.

Finally, take pride in the progress you've made and the dedication you've shown in mastering guitar modes.  This will give you confidence in your commitment to learning and growing as a musician and expand your repertoire.

As you continue to explore and create, may your love for music inspire and guide you to new heights.  Keep learning, keep playing, and most importantly, keep sharing the joy of music with the world.

To all your success,

Sincerely, Dwayne Jenkins

# Other Books From Dwayne Jenkins

**Learn Guitar Scale Theory:**

Dive deep into guitar scale theory with this easy to learn from, comprehensive guidebook.  An understanding of theory can add a rich vocabulary for both harmony and melody.

Learning guitar scale theory will help you expand your improvisation skills, enhance your scale vocabulary, and deepen your understanding of intervals.

**Learn To Play Rhythm Guitar**:

A comprehensive training course for learning chords, chord progressions, strumming, arpeggiated picking, and all things needed to be a great rhythm guitar player.

With a step-by-step system and your desire to learn, you'll be playing quickly and easily.  Before you know it, you will improve your musicianship, timing, and rhythm.

**Learn Guitar Chord Theory**:

Have you ever looked at notation and wondered what a Cadd9 chord is?  Or possibly a Gsus4?  If you have, this book explains what it is, how to create it, and how to use it.

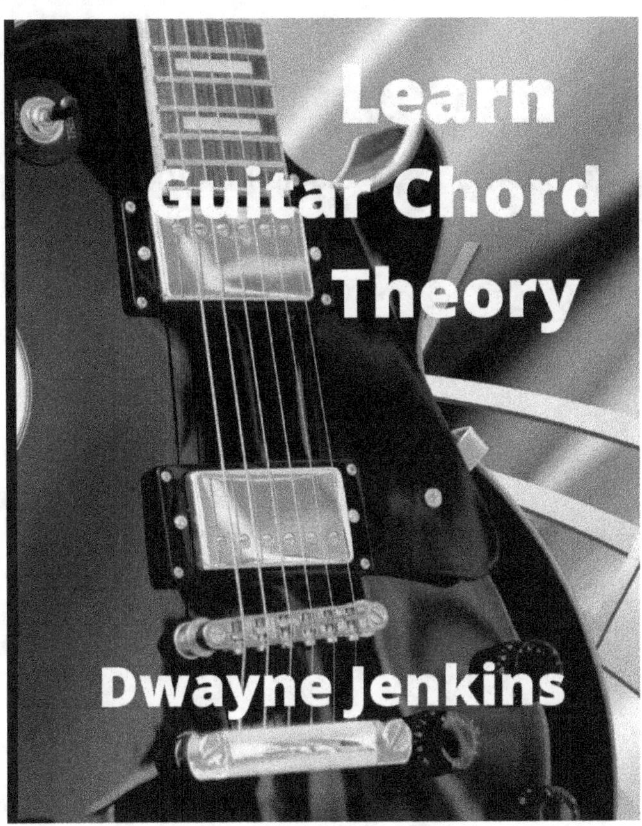


Learn Guitar Chord Theory is a comprehensive study guide on the inner workings of guitar chords.  Take the time to develop your chord vocabulary and mix it with a complete understanding of how they work, and you'll become a much better player.

132

All books are authored by Dwayne Jenkins, published by
Tritone Publishing, and are available worldwide.

Digital formats of all titles are also available for quicker learning.
Just download them onto your computer and start learning right
away.

Self-study is a great way to learn, as it allows you not only to go
at your own pace but also to develop self-discipline and time
management, which can benefit you in other areas of your life.

Also, check out Dwayne's Guitar Lessons video channel on
YouTube.  These are free lessons covering a wide range of
guitar topics.

Whether you are working on rhythm, lead, theory, or guitar
maintenance, it is all here in these lessons.  These are
available 24 hours a day, 7 days a week, 365 days a year.

If more help is needed, Dwayne also offers one-on-one
coaching, and he can be contacted through his website at
www.DwaynesGuitarLessons.com.

Best of luck, and be sure to have fun.

# About the Author

Dwayne Jenkins is a guitar teacher with a unique, engaging approach that helps students of all ages and skill levels enjoy playing the guitar and ukulele.  His enthusiasm and love for teaching shine through every lesson that he creates.

His lessons are designed to help you progress.  No matter your reason for learning, there will always be something in Dwayne's books and products to help you achieve your dreams.

So if you're a student looking to start or a student looking to further your education, be sure to get involved with Dwayne's guitar lessons and learn what so many people have already discovered: why learning to play the guitar is one of the most incredible things you can do for yourself.

## What Students Are Saying About Dwayne's Guitar Lessons

"Dwayne, thank you so much for everything you have taught me and done for me.  You are an amazing guitarist and wonderful teacher".  BJ.

"Dwayne, it has been a true pleasure to have you at our house each week! Ken & Trevor have learned so much through you and your teachings.  Thank you!" Lisa.

"Dwayne, thank you for being a great teacher and teaching me many great songs.  This is a skill that will last me a lifetime." Danielle.

"Dwayne, we want you to know we are honored to have you at the studio.  We appreciate all that you do and are grateful that we can leave you in charge." Angie & Wilson M.E.C.

"Dwayne, we are so glad you are our Teacher.  It's been three years already, can you believe it? Thank you again. You're the best!" Chelsey & Lucas.

"Dwayne, we are so glad that you are in our lives.  Chelsey & Lucas enjoy their time with you and look up to you.  Looking forward to another great year!" Love and best wishes, Ken & Sue.

"Dwayne, thank you so much for being not only an awesome guitar teacher but an awesome friend as well," Kayla.

"Dwayne, thank you so much for all the years of doing lessons. You have been very patient with my progress, helped me build confidence, and inspired me to pursue my dreams.  And in doing so, you have become a great friend." Jake.

"Dwayne, thank you for teaching Nick guitar so well.  He loves it and is getting quite good, fast. I'm amazed!" Jane.

"Dwayne, thank you so much for teaching me every Saturday, and not only teaching me guitar but also about life, and helping me with setting my goals.  You are a great teacher, mentor, and the best friend ever." Carson.

"There is no other person I would want to teach me a guitar! His 1-on-1 teaching makes learning guitar very personal & exhilarating.  He teaches at your pace and takes pride in what YOU want to learn.  The best part is that if Dwayne doesn't know a song a student wants to play, he takes time out of the week to learn it. His teaching comes to life in my performance and has progressed over the last 8 years. Words cannot describe how amazing a teacher, rockstar, and true friend Dwayne has become to me." Dominic.

# Resource Guide

## The Seven Modes of the Major Scale

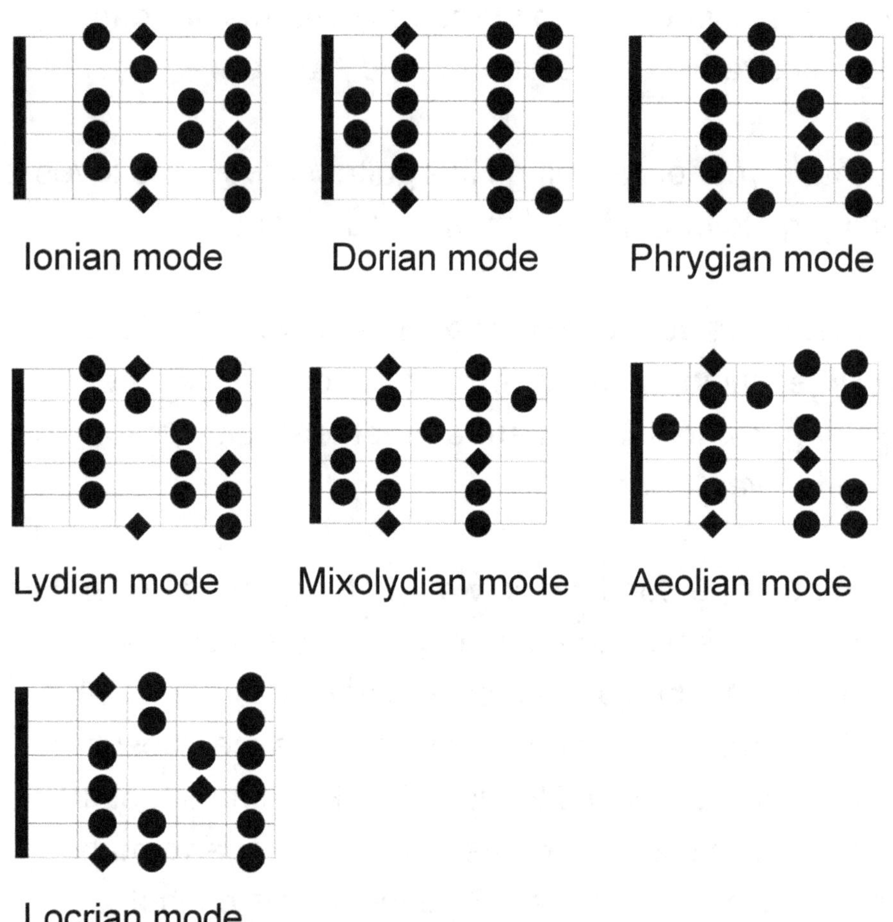

Ionian mode     Dorian mode     Phrygian mode

Lydian mode     Mixolydian mode     Aeolian mode

Locrian mode

Remember, these can be played anywhere along the fretboard.

Whole Step Formulas For the Seven Modes

1. Ionian mode:  W--W--H--W--W--W--H
2. Dorian mode:  W--H--W--W--W--H--W
3. Phrygian mode:  H–W–W–W–H–W–W
4. Lydian mode:  W–W–W–H–W–W–H
5. Mixolydian mode:  W–W–H–W–W–H–W
6. Aeolian mode: W–H–W–W–H–W–W
7. Locrian mode:  H–W–W–H–W–W–W

Note Interval Formulas For the Seven Modes

1. Ionian mode = Major:  1 2 3 4 5 6 7
2. Dorian mode = Minor: 1 2 b3 4 5 6 b7
3. Phrygian mode = Minor:  1 b2 b3 4 5 b6 b7
4. Lydian mode = Major:  1 2 3 #4 5 6 7
5. Mixolydian mode = Major:  1 2 3 4 5 6 b7
6. Aeolian mode = Natural Minor:  1 2 b3 4 5 b6 b7
7. Locrian mode = Diminished:  1 b2 b3 4 b5 b6 b7

The seven modes can be beneficial for both lead and rhythm guitar playing.  Understand the whole step and note interval formulas, and you'll enhance your guitar playing proficiency.

Resource Guide Continued

Common Triads Within the Modes

**Ionian:**  C major: (C-E-G), D minor: (D-F-A), E minor: (E-G-B),
F major: (F-A-C), G major: (G-B-D), A minor: (A-C-E),
B diminished: (B-D-F).

**Dorian:**  D minor: (D-F-A), E minor: (E-G-B), F major: (F-A-C),
G major: (G-B-D), Aminor: (A-C-E), B diminished: (B-D-F),
C major: (C-E-G).

**Phrygian:**  E minor: (E-G-B), F major: (F-A-C), G major:
(G-B-D), A minor:  (A-C-E), B diminished: (B-D-F), C major:
(C-E-G),
D minor: (D-F-A).

**Lydian:**  F major: (F-A-C), G major: (G-B-D), A minor: (A-C-E),
B diminished: (B-D-F), C major: (C-E-G), D minor: (D-F-A),
E minor: (E-G-B).

Remember, each mode contains a unique sequence of triads.
Knowing these intimately within each mode allows you to bring
out the specific modal character.

Resource Guide Continued

**Mixolydian**:  G major: (G-B-D), A minor: (A-C-E), B diminished: (B-D-F), C major: (C-E-G), D minor: (D-F-A), E minor: (E-G-B), F major:  (F-A-C).

**Aeolian:**  A minor: (A-C-E), B diminished: (B-D-F), C major: (C-E-G), D minor: (D-F-A), E minor: (E-G-B), F major: (F-A-C), G major: (G-B-D).

**Locrian:**  B diminished: (B-D-F), C major: (C-E-G), D minor: (D-F-A), E minor: (E-G-A), F major: (F-A-C), G major: (G-B-D), A minor: (A-C-E).

These are presented in the key of C major for easy learning. Take notice of the chords within each mode.  This same concept will follow in all keys you choose to play them in.

Major Triad = 1  3  5

Minor Triad = 1  b3  5

Diminished Triad = 1  b3  b5

Master the formula difference between the major, minor, and diminished triads for best results.

Resource Guide Continued

12-Bar Blues Progression:  I-IV-V Key of G major = G  C  D

The last measure is what's called a turnaround.  Utilizing the flat 5th chord.  Common in the blues, and takes you back to the root chord to start all over.

Practice this progression in different keys with different chords, always using the 1st, 4th, and 5th chords of each key.

The 12-bar blues progression is a great place to start creating and understanding chord progressions.  Hundreds of songs have been produced by it, and it is highly recommended that you learn and add them to your repertoire.

They are also a great place to start soloing over.  The reason is that the progression is already familiar to the ear, having been used in hundreds of songs over the years.

Also, once you have the basic triads down, look into learning about chord embellishments.  Adding other notes within the key to create chords like G7, Asus2, Cadd9, and so forth.

This will allow you to expand your chord vocabulary, learn to build on triads for more emotionally rich musical landscapes, and enhance both your rhythm and lead guitar playing.